ED MASHBURN

Kayak Fishing
the Northern Gulf Coast

Florida, Alabama, Mississippi, and Louisiana

4880 Lower Valley Road • Atglen, PA 19310

Designed by Molly Shields
Type set in Avance/Utopia Std

Maps used in this book are courtesy of
OpenStreetMap Contributors. Readers are directed
to openstreetmap.org for more information about
this most helpful service.
    All photos—except for those credited to other
photographers as they appear in the book—are by
the author.

ISBN: 978-0-7643-5411-3
Printed in China

Published by Schiffer Publishing, Ltd.
4880 Lower Valley Road
Atglen, PA 19310
Phone: (610) 593-1777;
Fax: (610) 593-2002
E-mail: Info@schifferbooks.com
Web: www.schifferbooks.com

For our complete selection of fine books on this
and related subjects, please visit our website at
www.schifferbooks.com. You may also write for a
free catalog.

Schiffer Publishing's titles are available at special
discounts for bulk purchases for sales promotions or
premiums. Special editions, including personalized
covers, corporate imprints, and excerpts, can be
created in large quantities for special needs. For
more information, contact the publisher.

We are always looking for people to write books on
new and related subjects. If you have an idea for a
book, please contact us at
proposals@schifferbooks.com.

This book is dedicated to my partner in kayak fishing and life, my wife, June. I treasure every minute we spend paddling and fishing the wonderful waters of the Gulf Coast and points beyond.

Contents

Preface

As a retired teacher, I see the world in educational terms, and I have tried to make this book much like the better textbooks I discovered in my years in the classroom. Each specific section in this book has a blank page at the end for notes, comments, questions, and information as it becomes needed. I hope that readers will be able to use this book as a planning guide for future trips to the Northern Gulf Coast.

Foreword

This book is not intended to be an exhaustive description of all kayak fishing possibilities that exist on the Northern Gulf Coast. No book could possibly relate every single possible place for kayak anglers to get on the water and catch some great fish.

Rather, this book is intended as a "kick starter" to get kayak anglers thinking about traveling to the Gulf Coast and as a plan book for future travels.

This book presents the information needed for kayak anglers to find out more and make good, solid plans for kayak fishing trips. Each angler will make specific plans and arrangements for trips, and that is the way things work out best.

So pick a spot, load up the 'yak and gear, and come on down. I hope to see you on the water.

So, What's So Special About the Northern Gulf Coast for Kayak Anglers?

It's going to be another great day on the Northern Gulf Coast for kayak anglers.

For kayak anglers, mobility is a big thing. Being able to load up the kayak, load up some gear, and then just . . . go. That is a big reason so many anglers are turning from big, expensive, hard-to-move powerboats and turning to kayaks—cheap, compact, and very easy to load, unload, and get on the water. And, most importantly, kayaks are very effective fishing craft.

It seems the Northern Gulf Coast of the USA is one of the very best places for kayak anglers—no matter where they call home—to locate and catch some truly amazing fish. Out-of-area kayak anglers can quickly and easily find themselves in some wonderful fishing on the Northern Gulf Coast, even if they are not familiar at all with the coast.

From Tallahassee, Florida, in the east to Lake Charles, Louisiana, in the west, kayak anglers have a world of fishing choices: freshwater, saltwater, or mixed. There are more kinds of fish to be caught here than just about any other place in the country.

There are some very fine choices for kayak anglers when they need to find places to stay on the Northern Gulf Coast—totally wild and rustic camp sites, modern, clean, inexpensive chain motels, or even palatial upscale beach front vacation homes—they are all on the Northern Gulf Coast.

And it is all easy to get to and then get on the water quickly. In this guide, I have tried to give a representative sample of the kinds of fishing to be done on the Northern Gulf Coast and specific locations to easily access the water. But rest assured, there are many, many more places to put the 'yak in and catch fish than I have covered here. That is part of the pleasure of kayak fishing the Northern Gulf Coast: No matter what state on the coast a kayak angler is in, there are always more spots to go fishing that very few other anglers know about. The Northern Gulf Coast is a kayak angler's paradise.

It's Not Just for Folks Who Live on the Coast

For a kayak angler who lives in the eastern or midwestern parts of the country, the Northern Gulf Coast—Florida, Alabama, Mississippi, and Louisiana—can be reached without a lot of pain, suffering, or expense. For much of the country north of the Gulf Coast, a kayak angler can drive for a day and be in a different world of warmer air, warmer water, and much more willing-to-bite fish.

There is plenty of water along the Northern Gulf Coast for kayak anglers.

When my family and I used to live in the Midwest, we would leave the St. Louis area early in the morning and be on the Gulf Coast by sunset. For much of the country a twelve-hour drive can make a huge difference in the world. Even for folks who live in places that can't reach the Gulf Coast in a day, it is still an easy trip, even if an overnight stay somewhere along the route has to be made. And of course kayak fishing is the cheapest way to go fishing short of standing on the shoreline and casting.

Kayak anglers from Atlanta, Cincinnati, St. Louis, Knoxville, Kansas City, Dallas, San Antonio, Charlotte, Charleston, and even Chicago ought to consider the Northern Gulf Coast a very doable destination—because it is.

Just imagine one of those cold, gray, nasty winter days in the upper Midwest—the sleet is changing to snow and the roads are starting to ice up and get slick. Sounds pretty grim, doesn't it?

Now picture this: A day's drive away the water is liquid, the air is soft and warm, the food is hot, spicy, and delicious, and the fish are biting.

If that does not make you think about loading up the 'yak and doing a road trip to the Northern Gulf Coast I guess nothing will.

Kayak anglers in winter can go from this . . .

What Kind of Kayaks

Many kayak anglers who are not yet regular visitors to the Gulf Coast may worry that their kayaks may not be suitable for fishing here. After all, there is a world of models, sizes, and forms of kayaks with lots of options and features. So which kayaks will work for fishing on the Gulf Coast?

Well, for Gulf Coast fishing from a kayak, I will state with no hesitation that the very best kayak for fishing here is . . . the one you have.

If you look at many of the photos in this book, you will see that a lot of the fish being caught in the photos are being caught by my family members or me, and we are

. . . to this in a single day's drive. So what's keeping you in the snow?

fishing from little old sit-in Wilderness Systems kayaks that have not been built nor sold for many years. However, these little old kayaks work quite well for many of our fishing trips on the coast—and they are paid for, too.

I even catch a lot of fish while fishing from wooden strip-built cruising kayaks that I make myself. These boats were not originally designed as fishing craft, but they work just fine for that purpose.

Of course, I have a top-of-the-line Hobie pedal kayak, and we have several other very nice designed-for-fishing kayaks that we use a lot. But the point is this—do not let the kind of kayak you have keep you from coming to the coast and catching some fish.

To be sure, some kayaks will work better for fishing than others. Kayaks designed and built for fishing will be more comfortable and more effective. But you can catch a lot of fish from any sort of kayak. It just needs to be down here with you in it.

Weather and Seasons of the Year

Make no mistake, the Northern Gulf Coast is not the tropics. In winter it gets chilly, but chilly is a relative thing. For us who live on the coast chilly is a night that drops below forty degrees. Many winter days will have mid-day temperatures of seventy-five or above. Even in the chilliest weather we get on the Gulf Coast we can still get on the water and catch fish in our kayaks. Kayak anglers need to come with good waterproof and wind-proof clothing and gear for winter trips. A little tip: I have found a very lightweight pair of neoprene waders to be absolutely wonderful for cool-weather kayak fishing trips. The waders keep you dry, and if you're dry you are probably going to be comfortable.

During the summer it is rare for daily temperatures to be higher than the lower nineties. However, the humidity can be brutal. When it is ninety degrees with ninety-five percent humidity it will wilt most kayakers. Kayak anglers can expect summertime thunderstorms on a daily basis. All along the coastline, when the first rumble of thunder is heard, anglers need to head to somewhere safe, like dry land. Most summer thunderstorms are violent but very short lasting, and the fishing after a storm dies down can be fantastic.

Yes, the weather can get rough on the coast.

Here is an important thing to keep in mind: kayak anglers need to come prepared with long-sleeved shirts and long pants and protective sunblock for summer trips.

Summer is the classic "go to the beach" season, and it is very nice here in summer. One of the biggest problems with summer kayak fishing on the Gulf Coast is that there are lots of other folks here, too—it can get crowded in some places. Another big problem here in summer is the sun. Light-complected folks must take precautions to protect against sunburn. The summer sun on the coast can burn a person badly in a remarkably short period of time, and a bad sunburn is a trip-killer. Long sleeves, long pants, and lots of sunblock are a good start. Face coverings and gloves are not bad ideas to prevent sunburn. Of course, the best way to combat summer sunburn is to fish early and late in the day—the fish seem to bite better then, anyway.

Spring on the Gulf Coast is very nice: the water is starting to warm; migratory fish like mackerel, cobia, and tarpon are starting to show up off the beaches; and the inshore fish really get started feeding up for spawning.

Now fall—I love fall on the Northern Gulf Coast. The air is not as hot as it was in summer, but it is still very comfortable. The water is still very warm, and the big fish are still here and feeding up heavily for their cool weather migration. Tourist season is over and many folks have gone back home, so there is a lot less pressure on the water. I love kayak fishing here in the fall . . .

Except for those big, bad storms that come with names like Erin, Opal, Ivan, and Katrina.

Hurricanes generally come in fall, and when they come, things on the coast get very, very bad. Of course, if you are a visiting kayak angler you do not need to worry:

Perhaps not the best day for kayak fishing on the coast.

the authorities will not let you come to the coast if a big storm is predicted. When a tropical storm is predicted to make landfall on the coast authorities shut down the highways for some distance inland and non-residents are turned back. That is a very good thing—you really do not want to be down here when a big storm comes in, as it is not fun at all. But, other than hurricanes, fall is the finest season of the year.

Food: Not Much Better Anywhere

One of the real attractions of the Northern Gulf Coast for kayak anglers who live in other less-blessed-with-food parts of the country is the good eating. I have eaten seafood in many parts of the world, and there is none better than can be found on the Gulf Coast of the US. Whether you like fish, oysters, crabs, shrimp, scallops, or calamari, it is all here, and it is all good.

In every little village along the coast, kayak anglers will find world class seafood cafes and restaurants which will provide wonderful dining. Every state on the Gulf

Give me oysters and beer for dinner every day of the year and I'll feel fine . . . .

A Gulf Coast classic: Po-boy sandwiches are so fine.

Coast has its own variety and style of making seafood gumbo, that dark, rich, spicy, wonderful Cajun meal in a bowl. It would be a good use of off-the-water time to experiment trying out gumbo in a variety of locations to see which state makes the best gumbo. (My favorite gumbo comes from South Alabama, around Coden and Dauphin Island, but that's just me.)

Of course, each state along the coast thinks its seafood is the best, and they are all right, of course, but we can't let the discussion of food go by without making comment about the food in Louisiana. There are more kinds of seafood cooking in Louisiana and more kinds of seafood to cook there than can be found anywhere else.

Also, I have got to mention that the barbecue on the coast is a mix of East Coast and Midwest barbecue techniques and sauces, along with a big portion of Deep South-style cooking. You can find vinegar-based Carolina style sauce, sweet sticky Memphis-Kansas City style sauce, and you can find white Alabama-style barbecue sauce—it's all here. We use pecan wood for smoking, and we take our grilling and smoking seriously.

Now, for a real treat try some slow-smoked fish—mullet is good and smoked cobia is prime. Smoked fish is a Gulf Coast specialty, and it is a wonderful thing to eat accompanied by a bottle of really cold beer.

My friends, if you come to the Gulf Coast and go around hungry then you're not trying hard enough to find the food—it is here.

How to Get Around: I-10—The Mother Road
The area covered by this book—from the Tallahassee region to Lake Charles—is more than 570 miles; it is a big, wide expanse of potential fishing spots. To drive straight from Florida to westernmost Louisiana, as covered in this book, will take more than eight hours.

We kayak anglers who hit the road looking for good fishing are in luck, though. Good, old, reliable I-10 provides safe, usually-rapid transport from east to west.

Get on I-10, the quickest way to get from here to there on the Gulf Coast.

Traffic can be rough on the Mother Road (I-10), but just go with it and don't get uptight.

There are driving options. Highway 98 runs along the water and it is a great kayak fishing road.

It is not nearly as fast as I-10, but Highway 98 is much better for kayak anglers who want to see the water.

Now, you have got to understand that I-10 gets lots of big truck traffic, and at certain pinch points along the way traffic can get painful. Make no mistake about it, driving I-10 is freeway driving.

Basically, the slow spots will be at Tallahassee and around Pensacola during rush hours, and around any major highway construction going on. Mobile, with its tunnels, is always slow, and on weekends and holidays I-10 in Mobile can be very bad. The Biloxi interchanges can be busy at rush hours and slow. New Orleans can be quite bad during rush hours, or in case of an accident, so be patient if you drive through the old Big Easy. If you are driving a car or truck with a non-Louisiana license my best advice is this: *slow down*. Even on I-10 out-of-state tags get stopped a lot in Louisiana.

For visiting kayak anglers who drive through these pinch points I would recommend trying to hit the bad spots either very early in the morning or very late at night. This is not always possible, but it can sure make the bad parts of a kayak fishing trip go better.

Other Coastal Roads

We've focused on I-10 as our point of departure for basic place-to-place transport on the Northern Gulf Coast, and that is logical—I-10 is the best way to get from here to there in the shortest amount of time. But sometimes we kayak anglers want to take our time and see what is really possible.

In most of the states covered there are other smaller and slower roads which parallel the coast and give kayak anglers some great opportunities to pull over, park, and slide the 'yak in for some fishing. When we get close to places we want to explore we must exit the fast lanes of I-10 and drive south on the smaller highways that lead to the water. There are lots of these smaller roads.

For example, my favorite road in all of the world is old Highway 98, which runs from eastern Northern Gulf Florida along the coast—often right next to the water—all the way to Pensacola. This old, mostly-two-lane highway provides kayak anglers with wonderful views and access to some prime kayak fishing water. There are more kayak fishing access spots from Highway 98 than a single kayak angler could ever visit in a long lifetime of fishing.

Of course, as Highway 98 approaches Panama City and the other white-sand beach parts of the state it gets much more clotted with traffic, but it still gives us kayak anglers an option which I-10 just can't. Hwy 98 and Hwy 90 run parallel to the water for almost the entire run of the coast from St. Marks, Florida, to the Mississippi/Louisiana border. Driving these roads will be much slower than running on I-10, but it will put anglers in much closer proximity to fishing water.

What Kind of Gear and Bait?

For many kayak anglers who have not been fishing on the coast before, there is a temptation to run out once the driving is over and the coast is in sight and buy up a lot of new "saltwater" fishing equipment, to buy a whole tackle box of new "saltwater" lures and tackle. That may not be necessary. Let's look at equipment and gear that will work for most kayak fishing situations on the Gulf Coast.

Any rod and reel that holds 200 yards of twenty-lb. line and has a very good and reliable drag system is adequate for most inshore fishing on the Gulf Coast. Bass anglers

Yes, we catch some fine fish from kayaks on the Northern Gulf Coast, like this red snapper.

with level-wind rigs that can be loaded with plenty of line are set to go. It is crucial that the reel holds at least 200 yards of line, because when a big redfish takes the bait and runs it usually will not stop in a few yards as freshwater bass do when hooked.

Spinning gear works fine, too. A good spinning reel loaded with twenty-lb. line—at least 200 yards of it—on a medium-weight rod is perfect for most inshore Gulf Coast fishing.

The Gulf Coast is not the place for ultra-light gear. Trying to use rods and reels that are too light and small is an invitation for heartbreak when that biggest fish of your life hits and runs and keeps on running and the line melts off the little reel and then goes "pop." Have a rig that is up to the job. Either mono or braid line works well.

There is no reason to buy the heavy, multi-hook and bead and swivel-equipped leaders that lots of Gulf Coast stores try to sell to visiting anglers. Most of the time a short twenty-in. section of twenty-five-lb. fluorocarbon line works quite well as a leader attached to the main line with a black swivel.

Fly rod anglers can have a world of fun on the Gulf Coast fishing from a kayak. Fly rods need to be at least five wt., but seven wt. is better—I use an eight wt. most of the time. The eight wt. rod allows me to throw bigger, bulkier flies a bit farther, which can be important.

Of course, for fishing out in the Gulf, where the *big* fish play, heavier gear is needed. I recommend waiting to buy any big water rods, reels, and other major investment equipment until you arrive on the coast. Find a good bait and tackle shop—there are several named in this book in the specific location chapters—and ask what kind of rig is needed for off-the-beach kayak fishing. Basically, it comes down to this: you need

And this is why we use steel leaders when fishing in the gulf: lots of sharp teeth in the saltwater.

a rod and reel—either spinning or level wind—that can handle twenty-five lb. line and a lot of it—again, at least 200 yards.

When fishing in the open Gulf, wire leaders are necessary because many of the fish that are caught have some very impressive dental equipment and mono leaders just will not last long.

The most important thing needed for kayak fishing in the open Gulf is a load of patience. The fish here are big and strong, and they will not come to the kayak quickly or easily when hooked. In fact, most of the time when fishing in the open Gulf off the beaches, kayak anglers will be taken for a "kayak sleigh ride" by hooked fish. This can be alarming at first, but it is really a lot of fun to be pulled around by a big fish. Just be patient with big fish and let the weight of the kayak being towed about wear the fish down.

One important piece of equipment the beyond-the-breakers kayak angler needs is a fish bag or ice chest to keep caught fish in. The bag—a heavy duty soft-side ice chest—or a traditional hard-side ice chest will keep the caught fish cold and in good shape for cleaning and cooking, but it is also much safer for the kayaker.

DO NOT PUT CAUGHT FISH ON A STRINGER! This is the best way known to man to come in very close contact with some big, hungry, aggressive sharks. Having big sharks approach your kayak is interesting at any time, but having a big shark come up and take the fish from a stringer and then start pulling your kayak backward until the stringer breaks or is bitten in two is not much fun. Get a good secure ice chest to keep the fish in.

Choosing bait and lures is not as difficult as it might appear. Basically, it comes down to this: everything that swims on the Gulf Coast loves live bait. Especially everything eats live shrimp. Everything that swims in the open Gulf eats live or frozen bait like cigar minnows, Spanish sardines, or mullet. All of this live bait can be found at area bait and tackle shops, and the frozen bait can be found at any of the area's big box stores or tackle shops.

Choosing lures is a bit more involved. But here is something to help: most coastal fish—especially redfish—will strike any bait or lure that a freshwater bass will take.

Expect to meet "Mr. Tooth" while kayak fishing on the Gulf—they're really not so bad.

Topwaters work, spinnerbaits work, and especially jigs with soft plastic grub bodies work very well for redfish.

Now, a very important point for visiting freshwater anglers to keep in mind: saltwater will rust and corrode almost everything made of metal if it is not rinsed off. Especially those favorite reels—rinse and lube them carefully after each use, or you will be unhappy to find rust and corrosion on the equipment a month or so after you get back home. This is important—rinse the saltwater off. And whatever else you do, do not let the reels get in the sand of the beach. A sandy reel is a dead reel. It is very difficult to get fine, very hard sand out of a reel, and nothing sounds worse or functions more poorly than a reel with sand in the works.

Out-of-State Fishing Licenses

Before we can start thinking about the bait and lures and launch spots we want to use when fishing on the Northern Gulf Coast, we have to make sure that we are totally legal. It is very easy to make a connection with each state you visit and buy your out-of-state license online or over the phone. Here is the most up-to-date information about out-of-state licenses and requirements and fees:

Out of State License Fees

Florida
Contact Florida Fish and Wildlife Conservation Commission online or with their mobile app.
myfws.com/license
12 month - $47.00
7-day trip - $30.00
3-day trip - $17.00

Alabama
www.outdooralabama.com
Annual non-resident:
Louisiana - $90.10
Florida - $48.45
all other states- $49.25

Trip non-resident:
Louisiana - $27.30
Florida - $30.10
all other states - $27.30

Mississippi
www.mdwfp.com/license.fishing.license.aspx
Annual non-resident - $30.00 plus $4.29 fee
3-day non-resident trip - $15.00 plus $3.29 fee

Louisiana
Department of Wildlife and Fisheries, State of Louisiana
www.wlf.louisiana.gov/licenses/fishing
Non-resident basic license - $60.00
Non-resident basic fishing trip, 1-day - $5.00
Non-resident saltwater season - $30.00
Non-resident saltwater, 1-day trip - $17.50

So now we have got a pretty good idea what kind of place and what kind of fishing await kayak anglers who bring their paddle boats to the Northern Gulf Coast. Let's look at specific locations kayak anglers need to think about as possible destinations.

But be sure of this: there are many, many more great fishing spots along the Gulf Coast not mentioned in this book that are just waiting for kayak anglers to come and explore.

Also, visiting kayak anglers who do not want to bring their own personal kayaks with them on a vacation can find rental kayaks at many of the locations covered in this book. It is probably best to bring and use your own 'yak, but for a first trip feeling your way around using a rental kayak can be a good introduction to fishing on the coast.

On just about any Gulf Coast bayou shrimp boats will be seen.

Gear for Gulf Coast Kayak Anglers

For kayak anglers who plan on fishing trips to the Northern Gulf Coast, some gear which may not already be on the kayak should be part of the effort.

1. First and foremost, a well-fitting personal flotation device (PFD) is the most important single piece of equipment for coastal kayak anglers, and it must be worn at all times when the kayak is in use, especially in open Gulf waters. This is serious, folks—have a PFD and wear it.

2. An extended kayak warning flag. This allows powerboat captains to see kayakers in rough water conditions.

3. Rod and reel tie downs. When launching a kayak off the beach, rods and reels must be secured to the kayak. In case of a roll-over, the rod leash can prevent total equipment loss.

4. A good pair of fishing pliers. These need to be solid, strong pliers with a good line/hook cutter. It may become necessary to remove a hook that finds the wrong place to lodge—like a finger or arm—and a good pair of pliers makes the painful task of hook removal much easier.

5. For winter trips, a set of waterproof garments can help keep an angler on the water. The best waterproofs have hoods and big, roomy pockets.

6. For winter trips, a pair of lightweight neoprene fishing waders help keep a kayaker dry and warm.

7. For summer and fall trips, a set of lightweight long sleeve and full-length pants for sun protection. Gulf Coast summer sun is brutal and angler cover is necessary. A big full brim hat is best; baseball caps leave a lot of skin exposed.

8. A good sharp fishing knife in a secure holster.

9. Lots of drinking water. Even in winter kayakers go through a lot of liquid on a trip.

10. A waterproof camera for taking pictures of the big fish that will be caught.

Notes

FLORIDA

There's nothing like a Florida Gulf Coast sunrise to get a kayak angler going.

Actually, there are *two* Floridas examined in this book. There is the eastern part of the Florida Northern Gulf Coast and the much different western end of the Sunshine State's Northern Gulf Coast. We call these two very different stretches of land the Forgotten Coast and the Emerald Coast.

On the eastern end—the Forgotten Coast—there is a lot of superb kayak fishing water, some wonderful wild areas—and not much else. And that is why I love this region so much. From the coast south of Tallahassee until Panama City there are a few small towns, some villages, and no high rise developments at all. This is probably the least developed part of Florida. There are a few sandy beaches, so the area has been left in pretty much its primal state— which, again, is why I love this area.

Visiting kayak anglers will find lots of bayous and creeks—most of the streams are spring-fed and clear. There are massive areas of salt marsh and tidal influenced creeks. And of course there are lots and lots of fish that do not receive much fishing pressure and so are usually willing to bite kayak anglers' offerings.

There are some first class kayak shops in the Tallahassee area, and visiting kayak anglers will be able to find any needed parts, repairs, or equipment easily.

As kayak anglers move toward the west down the Northern Gulf Coast the situation changes. From Panama City all the way to the Alabama state line there are lots of superb white sand beaches and clear, emerald water. And lots of people. There really is a big difference between the two ends of the Florida Northern Gulf Coast. However, the important thing is they are both *good*!

Kayak fishing from the white sand beaches of the Northern Gulf Coast can be very rewarding. In fact, some of the best beyond-the-breakers kayak fishing in the world happens in the Destin–Navarre Beach–Pensacola Beach stretch. Kayak anglers can park the car, unload the 'yak, launch through the surf, and be hooked up with massive big game fish in a very short period of time on good days.

A wide range of great fish can be caught from kayaks on the Florida Gulf Coast, such as this small mahi-mahi.

Along with the good fishing in this part of Florida comes lots and lots of development. High rises and lots of traffic must be anticipated.

What Kinds of Kayak Fishing?

Kayak anglers on the Northern Gulf Coast of Florida have a very wide range of fishing venues to select from. There are some absolutely gorgeous clear spring-fed rivers which offer fine bass and other freshwater fishing for kayak anglers. There is classic small bayou creek fishing in many of the salt marshes east of Panama City. There are large, clear, grass-bed bays which offer wonderful topwater fishing for reds and specks. Of course, there is also off-the-beach fishing for big game species.

There are massive bays which offer fishing of every kind, from freshwater bass, bream, catfish, and striped bass in cool weather to fishing around structures in the bay itself for reds, sheepshead, mangrove snapper, and flounder.

Then there are the passes which lead to the Gulf, where kayak anglers can expect to encounter everything from Spanish and king mackerel to big jacks, to big reds, to cobia in migration season, to pompano, to . . . lots of fish are in the Florida passes.

In short, if you can't find something to fish for from your kayak in the Florida Northern Gulf waters you are probably not going to find it anywhere.

The start of a Florida Gulf Coast kayak fishing trip—fun ahead.

Housing for Visitors

Here again we are looking at two different worlds. On the eastern end of the Florida Northern Gulf Coast visiting kayak anglers will probably want to look for motels and other housing arrangements around Crawfordville—it is the only town of much size other than Tallahassee in this area, and Crawfordville has a wide range of different motels and other places to stay.

Ed Ball State Park, at the head of Wakulla River, outside Crawfordville, has a very nice hotel which is a converted private lodge. This is a wonderful place for visiting kayak anglers to stay, and it is quite close to the Wakulla River and other great fishing spots.

As we move westward toward Panama City the options widen considerably. From Panama City to Pensacola there are housing choices of all kinds, and some of the smaller beach communities have some very nice beach condos and rental houses which give visiting kayak anglers very quick access to the beach and beyond-the-breakers fishing.

Other Things to Do

For those who come to the eastern end of the Florida Northern Gulf Coast you had better like fishing—there is not much else to do. There are some very nice tours and rides on the upper Wakulla River on pontoon boats that sail out of Ed Ball State Park, and Tallahassee is not far—it is a college town, and there are plenty of entertainment possibilities there. It is fun to drive through the St. Marks Wildlife Refuge and see all of the birds and animals which don't pay passing cars any attention.

As we go west toward Panama City, massive Tyndall Air Force Base gives visitors the chance to see some of the country's most modern and very impressive military aircraft in action. Many of the planes can be seen from the highway as it passes through the base property.

From Panama City to Pensacola along Highways 98 and 90 there are many shopping centers and parks for non-anglers to enjoy and kayak anglers to endure.

In Pensacola visitors can look through the Naval Aviation Museum at Naval Station Pensacola and see some very impressive displays of naval aircraft through the years. And one of the very coolest non-fishing things to do is to watch the Blue Angels flight team as they run through their show routines during mid-week practices over the naval air station—it is amazing the things these planes and pilots can do.

And of course there are always the beaches. It is very satisfying to just lie on some of the finest soft white sand in the world and listen to the surf roll in.

The Gulf Coast of Florida is quite simply a magical place for kayak anglers and the families of those anglers. This is really a prime location for family vacations that also include superb kayak fishing choices.

It is fun to kayak to a good spot and then wade fish for some fast action.

Notes

Great Kayak Fishing Site 1

St. Marks National Wildlife Refuge Area, Wakulla County, Florida

General Site Information

This is the easternmost location of this book's focus, and it is one of the very best locations for kayak anglers. The St. Marks National Wildlife Refuge Area is a vast land of bayous, small creeks, larger rivers, and open exposure to the Gulf of Mexico.

The area of Florida's coast where the St. Marks Refuge area is located is known as the "Forgotten Coast," because it has not suffered the rampant overdevelopment of other coastal areas of Florida. This is a beautiful and wild part of Florida and it is perfect for kayak anglers.

The St. Marks National Wildlife Refuge area does not display the white sandy beaches of Florida farther to the west. This is limestone, oyster shell bottom, and marsh grass territory, and the fishing for kayak anglers is very good.

St. Marks National Wildlife Refuge gives kayak anglers the chance to catch inshore fish, such as redfish, speckled trout, flounder, Spanish mackerel, and sheepshead, and also larger game fish such as black drum, bull reds, tarpon (in season), and sharks.

Kayak anglers need to come prepared for a wide range of possible opponents. Medium weight spinning gear is standard equipment here. A seven-foot rod with a reel that holds 200 yards of twelve- to fifteen-lb. line is good. Baitcasting gear of similar weight is fine. Fly rod anglers need to use nine wt. or even ten wt. rods. There are some big, strong fish at St. Marks, and too light a fly rod just will not work well when something big takes an offered fly. Fly reels need to have a good drag system and lots of backing line.

A wide range of lures work well here, but most kayak anglers use soft plastic bodies on jigs. The scented GULP! products are good, but the fish do not mind eating up the regular soft plastics, too. Top water fishing with walk-the-dog-type plugs early and late

The oyster reefs of St. Marks produce lots of big speck trout for kayak anglers.

Some gorgeous bayous and creeks offer great kayak fishing in St. Marks.

can be very exciting. Fly anglers will do well with light colored poppers and gurglers, and chartreuse and white clouser type subsurface flies work very well, especially on the big speckled trout.

For best results day in and day out it is hard to beat a live shrimp fished under a popping cork—this advice will be repeated many times in this book. It is just very hard to beat a favorite food of all inshore species for bait, and everything that swims the Northern Gulf Coast loves to eat live shrimp.

Fly anglers have good results with shrimp-looking flies for reds and specks at St. Marks.

Here's the real deal: Live shrimp are the best and most reliable bait all along the Gulf Coast.

St. Marks Lighthouse is still working to keep boaters from getting lost.

Most kayak anglers will choose to launch at the lighthouse on the refuge land to fish the open waters of the mouth of the St. Marks River and the associated oyster bars, but there is great small bayou fishing in most of the smaller creeks and bayous criss-crossing the Refuge area. Most of these smaller streams will require either a portage or a kayak cart to reach the best waters—some of these bayous are a long, long walk from the nearest parking areas.

You never know what you will catch from a kayak at St. Marks—like this spiny boxfish puffer.

How to Access the Area

Reaching St. Marks from I-10 is not too hard, but depending on the time of day traffic through Tallahassee can be tough.

Driving Directions:

1. From I-10, take Exit 199 at Tallahassee on to Hwy 27 South Monroe Street.

2. Stay on Hwy 27 (Monroe St.) to junction into Hwy 363 South Woodville Hwy.

3. Take Hwy 363 - Woodville Hwy south to junction with Hwy 98.

4. Take Hwy 98 east to the refuge entrance—you will cross the St. Marks River—then turn right on Lighthouse Road.

Total distance from I-10: about twenty-five miles

Tallahassee is not a large city, and except for extreme rush hour traffic it is usually quite easy to move through the city and out to the very rural area south toward St. Marks. St. Marks is only twenty-five miles south of Tallahassee, so this is not a particularly grueling drive for kayak anglers.

Once the Refuge Area is reached on Highway 98, kayak anglers will want to drive on Lighthouse Road all the way to the lighthouse at the end of the road. This is a wonderful drive and all kinds of wildlife will be seen. When the end of the road at the lighthouse is reached, kayak anglers have a sixty-foot carry to the water where kayaks can be launched. Fishing begins immediately. One of the very best places for kayak anglers is Long Bar, which is easily visible at low tide just about 150 yards off the launch area at the lighthouse. There are very many oyster bars at the mouth of the St. Marks River at the lighthouse and they are all good for fishing.

For visiting anglers who have never fished waters with oysters before, the best advice we can provide is wear good, solid water shoes! Not flip-flops! Oyster shells have extremely sharp edges and bare feet will be cut badly from walking on oyster shells.

A Little Fish Story

The afternoon sun was beating down and the breeze—well, the breeze was somewhere else. It was hot and still, and the effort of pedaling my kayak even the short distance out to Long Bar from the beach at the old white lighthouse sent sweat running down my face. I wondered if the fishing would make the discomfort from the heat and humidity worth it.

Gulls and terns called as they flew over, looking for a fish supper, and the tall structure of the St. Marks lighthouse stood guard over the mouth of the St. Marks River as it entered Apalachee Bay and the open Gulf. Even with the uncomfortable heat it was easy to see how beautiful this wonderful fishing spot was.

Mullet were jumping, and here and there the water swirled as big things chased little things. The water here at the mouth of the St. Marks River was alive with fish of all kinds.

Fly fishing Long Bar off St. Marks Point can produce some great fish for kayak anglers.

My wife, who almost always makes the best choices when it comes to choosing fishing spots, chose the seaward end of Long Bar to fish with live shrimp, and I took the middle parts of the extended bar. This easy-to-reach oyster bar is really quite long—a good quarter of a mile from end to end—that's why it is called Long Bar. I was fishing with soft plastic grubs on ¼-oz. jigheads—a standard Gulf Coast inshore rig—and I expected to find success with this tried and true offering.

It only took a few minutes of work in the hot, hot sun and I heard my wife call for my help landing a big redfish. I know my place in the world, so I started a quick retrieve of my jig so I could paddle down to help with her fish, and so she could show off and brag about who caught the first fish—again. This sort of thing happens quite often when we go fishing.

But my jig never made it back to the kayak. A vicious strike and a powerful run told me my wife was not the only person closely attached to a nice redfish. At this point I forgot all about how hot it was—I was having too much fun. The first run of a hooked redfish, no matter the size of the fish, is always something to admire. My reel gave line, the drag screeched a little, and then I got the fish coming my way . . . .

I fought my fish and finally got it by the kayak—obviously this was a legal slot-sized red, and since we were looking for a fresh fish supper this red went into the ice chest behind my seat.

As I paddled toward my wife—she had already worked her red in and landed it by herself; she is really very capable of doing such things—something very big smashed a school of mullet that was cruising along the steeper side of Long Bar.

Redfish are very often caught by kayak anglers at St. Marks around the bars and channels.

Mullet were literally knocked out of the water up on to the dry oyster shell surface of Long Bar as something about six feet long with a long tail, upright dorsal fin, and a bad attitude crashed into the school of mullet again and again. It was a bad time and place to be a mullet.

My wife and I agreed as we watched the carnage that we did not need to make an acquaintance with a big, hungry bull shark such as this.

With two fine redfish in the cooler for supper we could concentrate on just having fun, and with the several speckled trout and redfish that came to play with us we had a wonderful afternoon and evening fishing at St. Marks and Long Bar. When the summer sun moved closer to the horizon we decided it was time to head in, and since we had not paddled more than a half mile from our launch site we made our return in a few minutes—another big advantage of fishing the St. Marks area is long paddles are not required to catch all the fish desired.

I cleaned the reds when we reached the beach and we put them on ice for the trip back home to the fish camp.

And yes, the redfish were wonderful fresh off the grill—you just can't beat redfish on the half shell for some good eating after some great catching.

Special Considerations

The St. Marks National Wildlife Refuge area is quite undeveloped, meaning that places to stay and places to eat are scarce. When using the St. Marks Refuge Area for put-in and take-out, kayak anglers need to bring everything they might need with them—including water. There are no services other than restrooms and information at the refuge area's office and information center on Lighthouse Road.

Once in the refuge there are restroom facilities at the picnic area on Lighthouse Road.

Kayak anglers should be prepared once in the refuge area to see eagles, ospreys, all kinds of wading birds, and even whooping cranes when they migrate south in winter. It is a world class destination for birders.

Also, kayak anglers will see some of the biggest alligators to be found anywhere. Some massive 'gators live in the refuge, and they can be impressively shocking when they crash into the water as a kayaker paddles past. The gators are not interested in kayak anglers, but they do not like to be approached too closely.

There are plenty of gators to be seen at St. Marks. Leave them alone and they will not bother kayak anglers.

Kayak anglers can expect to meet with some of the refuge's smaller and more annoying residents, too. Mosquitoes and deer flies can be very bad here at times, so kayak anglers need to come prepared with good bug repellent, and long-sleeved shirts are a good idea. The bugs can be pretty bad.

The closest campground is a nice county-operated facility just outside the refuge entrance west on Hwy 98. It is almost never filled with campers, and there is a boat ramp on the campgrounds on the St. Marks River. Visiting kayak anglers who stay in the campground could launch at the ramp and paddle either upstream or downstream on the St. Marks River and catch some good freshwater fish and see some wonderful wildlife, too.

There is a restaurant/bar just across the St. Marks River on Highway 98 West. There are motels toward Crawfordville past the Wakulla River (more on this wonderful place later), and Crawfordville has the full range of big box stores and chain restaurants. Just west of Crawfordville, on Highway 98 at Medart, is a quite good barbecue place, Hamaknocker's. Their half chicken special is a good buy and some good eating, too.

There is a very nice bed and breakfast—Sweet Magnolia Inn (850-925-7670)— at the tiny town of St. Marks. At Ed Ball State Park the old private lodge has been converted into a very nice hotel and restaurant. Kayak anglers who fish the St. Marks area and the Wakulla River could do much worse than spend some time at the park's lodge.

Local Sources of Information
The Wilderness Way
Rob Baker
850-877-7200
www.thewildernessway.net
Rob Baker and his staff at The Wilderness Way give kayak anglers a wide range of services, from sales to repair of kayaks. This is also the place to locate guide services and shuttle services for any of the area waters.

Quite simply, The Wilderness Way is just about the very best kayak shop to be found on the entire Gulf Coast—they are good folks. This place is very highly recommended to kayak anglers.

St. Marks Outfitters
850-510-7919
redfish@stmarksoutfitters.com
Mike McNamara and his staff offer visiting kayak anglers many services, from advice to guided trips, including larger boat transfer of kayaks and anglers to remote locations for fishing. They will tailor trips to fit the needs of kayak anglers.

Forgotten Coast Kayak Anglers
FCKA is an online forum of area kayak anglers who provide a lot of good advice for folks not familiar with the area. This is a good place to introduce yourself before a trip and get good up-to-the-minute advice about where to go and how to fish the St. Marks area.

Great Kayak Fishing Site 2
Wakulla River, Wakulla County, Florida

One of the prettiest rivers anywhere, the Wakulla River is perfect for kayak anglers.

This Wakulla River barred owl could not decide which kayaker to look at.

General Site Information

I can't be totally objective about the Wakulla River. It is one of my favorite places in the world. I wish I were in my kayak floating down the Wakulla River right now.

The Wakulla River is a very short river; it runs only about eight miles from its headwaters at Ed Ball State Park outside Crawfordville until it joins with the St. Marks River at the tiny town of St. Marks. From this point the joined rivers run into Apalachee Bay and the Gulf.

However, in its short run to the Gulf the Wakulla River presents kayak anglers with one of the most beautiful streams to be found anywhere. Totally spring fed, the Wakulla usually has very clear water, allowing sight fishing and location of good fish-holding structure. Vast beds of native water plants provide great cover for a wide range of fish and other animals.

Many side spring runs can lead kayakers up perfectly clear feeder streams to places where springs deliver vast amounts of clear, cool water to the river's flow. In fact, the river stays basically the same temperature all year round because of the massive springs. Fishing stays good year round, too.

And animals and birds? This is one of the best places in the world to see manatees, those massive, slow-moving, gentle giants that are making a good comeback in Florida waters from their previously threatened numbers. Alligators are also common, as are water turtles.

Deer and wild hogs are common here, and bears are not uncommon, though they are rarely seen.

Some amazing birds will be seen when kayakers are on the Wakulla: eagles, ospreys, herons of many kinds, ducks by the thousands in migration times, warblers, and other smaller but brilliantly colored birds call the Wakulla River area home.

And the fishing? For freshwater and saltwater species the Wakulla can be very good.

The Wakulla is a stream of many personalities. In the upper reaches, where the river exits the fenced and totally protected area of Ed Ball State Park and can then be accessed by anglers, freshwater species such as largemouth bass, redbelly bream—often called stumpknockers locally—bluegill bream, and other freshwater fish are dominant. A really nice fish that calls the Wakulla River home is the Suwannee bass. This little sub-species of largemouth is not native to the Wakulla. It was unofficially introduced to the river from its native waters, the Suwanee River some miles to the east, probably by anglers who released their live catch. The Suwannee is a small bass—a two-pounder is a big one—but it looks and fights like a smallmouth bass, and there is not much higher praise I can give a freshwater fish than to compare it to a smallmouth bass.

There are some very big largemouth bass in the Wakulla, but they did not get big by being stupid. To hook up with a big Wakulla bass expect to make long casts, and expect to lose many more big ones than you catch. There are lots of grass, weeds, and

Lots of gorgeous and aggressive largemouth bass can be found and caught in the Wakulla River.

This Wakulla River bass came on a homemade lure cast with a homemade rod from a homemade kayak.

Suwanee bass in the Wakulla River are small, but they fight hard, like Deep South smallmouth bass.

logs in the water for big fish to break off on. Also, twelve-lb. test line is about as heavy as you can get away with—anything heavier and the bass will see it and leave the lure or bait alone.

I have had excellent results on the Wakulla with a wide range of soft plastic lures such as flukes, worms, and frogs. I like to rig these soft plastics weightless and weedless. I cast into backwater spots that have good shade cover and I let the lure slowly sink. Watch the line! When it twitches set the hook. I also like to cast these same weedless and weightless soft plastics far back over floating weeds and then hop the lure across the surface. When a Wakulla River bass blasts up through the weeds to devour a lure it is a special moment.

By the way, these Wakulla River largemouth are the most beautiful largemouth bass I have ever seen. They are healthy, dark, and brilliantly colored.

There are many side channels and islands which lie in the course of the Wakulla River's run, and kayak anglers will do well to explore these side channels and offshoots because they often hold fish. Cast ahead of the kayak as you progress up these side waters.

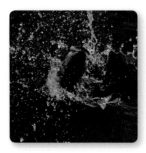

Wakulla River bass strike hard and fight harder—lots of fun for kayak anglers.

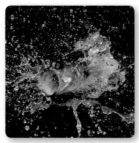

Clear Wakulla River water allows kayak anglers to sight fish for good bass.

From the Highway 98 bridge to St. Marks the Wakulla River has good wintertime sheepshead fishing.

As the river flows southward the range of species broadens. Saltwater species such as redfish, mullet, sheepshead, and blue crabs start to show up as the river approaches the Highway 98 crossing. In fact, the Highway 98 Bridge is a favorite sheepshead fishing spot in winter for anglers who cast live fiddler crabs for big black-and-white sheepshead below the bridge. When the river moves farther south toward the junction with the St. Marks River it becomes totally saltwater oriented, with redfish, flounder, sheepshead, and other saltwater fish present.

How to Access the Area

Getting to the Wakulla is easy; just follow the same directions as presented earlier for the St. Marks National Wildlife Refuge. Exit off I-10, make your way through Tallahassee, then go south until the junction with Hwy 98 is reached. Then, instead of going east toward the refuge, go west on Hwy 98. This will cross the Wakulla River in less than ten miles.

At the Hwy 98 crossing kayak anglers can turn on to a short dirt access road which will lead to the public launch below the Hwy 98 Bridge. The fee for launching is $5.00 and it is worth every penny.

T-n-T Hideaway is a first rate kayak rental and shuttle outfitter which can be found alongside the public launch area. These are the same folks who operate The Wilderness Way kayak shop, and they are good people to help arrange shuttle services, or just to provide good advice for fishing the river.

Many kayak anglers use the shuttle service to take them and their 'yaks back upstream to the Hwy 267 crossing, where they can put in and fish and float their way downstream to the Hwy 98 crossing and pull out. The float will take from a few hours if you paddle it straight to an all-day trip if you fish it right.

I prefer to launch my kayak at the Hwy 98 crossing and paddle or pedal upstream, fishing as I go. When I get enough fishing I simply turn around and float back to the launch area.

Anglers and floaters need to be aware that since the Wakulla is a true tidewater river its flow is greatly influenced by the state of the tide downstream at the Gulf. If

The Wakulla River is a great place to see manatees—very impressive animals up close from a kayak.

All kinds of Florida wildlife will be seen when kayak fishing on the Wakulla River.

the tide at the Gulf is high it tends to hold the flow of the river's water up, so the current slows way down. In this case, if there is a southern breeze floaters and anglers may find themselves moving back upstream.

If the tide is low it allows the river to empty out freely and the river's flow will be stronger and floaters will move a bit faster.

A Little Fish Story

The water of the Wakulla River was slowly making its way toward the junction with the St. Marks River a few miles below my launch place. The water was clear—I could see the bottom easily in six feet of water and even deeper as I started my paddle upstream.

"Now this is pretty neat," I thought.

When I had paddled a couple hundred yards upstream I heard the rattling laughter of a pileated woodpecker shattering the early morning stillness of the river and the quiet of the departing night off in the densely wooded bottoms. Then I saw a large shape flowing very quickly toward me over the water of the river. As it drew nearer—and this took only a moment—the white head and tail of an adult bald eagle flashed past me no more than thirty feet over my head as the great bird sped downstream.

"Wow, that was really cool!" I said quietly.

I paddled a few hundred yards farther along and my wife in her kayak silently but frantically motioned me to come closer and look up. As I neared the still deeply shaded side of the river I strained my eyes to witness what she wanted me so badly to see. I was trying too hard. There, not very far at all, maybe ten feet above me, was a barred owl, still holding to his night perch and swiveling his head to look first at my wife and then at me. We watched the owl and it watched us until we decided to move on. The owl never left—he may still be there.

"That was really nice," I thought, and said so to my wife.

My wife paddled on ahead of me—she likes to explore on her own, but I like to fish, and fishing is a deliberate game.

Over on the other bank in a patch of first light sunshine, a small five-foot-long alligator was sunning himself, and when I paddled toward him he thrashed off his log and into the clear water with a splash; that made me smile and realize that this morning was indeed a very good morning.

I secured my kayak's bow line to the end of an ancient cypress tree limb that had fallen in the water so I could rest and fish this nice, deep pocket of water. I was changing my lure when I glanced over the side of my kayak and saw a large part of the bottom of the river detach itself and float gently upward toward me. This thing was huge, and I was spooked for a moment. Things this big are not supposed to just float up off the bottom like this, especially when I'm in the vicinity.

But as this massive shape came closer to me and my kayak, I realized that a manatee was coming to wish me a good morning. The broad, flat, ugly-cute face broke the surface within a paddle's reach of me and the small beady eyes looked at me and my kayak, then the manatee made a "whuff, whuff" sound and sank back down into her deep sleeping water. And then I noticed her much smaller baby, which came even closer to me and my kayak. This baby manatee was big, but nothing like the massive momma. The baby came up beside my kayak, "whuffed" at me a couple times, and then gently sank to join momma on the bottom for another nice manatee nap.

"That was the coolest thing possible," I said quietly.

Just upstream from where the manatees were sleeping was an old, falling-down-from-neglect wooden boat dock. The dock had been there for a long, long time, and

Some really big Florida bass call the Wakulla River home, but they are not easy to catch.

its wooden posts were still in position, even though most of the planking had long since been washed away.

Such places are impossible for me to pass up when I have a fishing rod in my hand. I made a long cast; my soft plastic lure splashed into the water just off the outside piling—one of very few perfect casts I make during any fishing trip.

I let the lure sink, and then I noticed my line give the slightest little twitch. I took up all the slack and made a good solid hookset. But nothing happened—my line and lure just held solid. But then the line began to move, and I had a big, dark, gorgeous Wakulla River largemouth bass dancing with me. We danced briefly, but I managed to move the fish away from the dock and into open water. Then I reached down and firmly grasped the bass by the lower jaw and lifted her from the water.

Now, if one of my friends had caught this bass I would have said it was a four-pounder, maybe. But since I caught it, I would swear then and I will swear now that it was five and a half pounds, maybe six.

And as I held the fine fish for a couple quick photos and then a good safe life-saving release I knew that I had been lucky enough to see another morning on the Wakulla River, seeing so many wonderful things, and that catching this wonderful fish really was the best thing that happened on this day at this fine place.

Special Considerations

Now, here's the bad part. Since the Wakulla River is only twenty miles from Tallahassee it gets extremely heavy use by a wide range of people—many of whom are total yahoos—on weekends and holidays. I once made the mistake of trying to float and fish the Wakulla on a summertime holiday weekend and it was disgusting.

Please try to plan fishing trips for spring and fall, or if during summer, middle-of-the-week trips.

Also, the earlier you can get on the water the longer you will have to fish in peace. Even on midweek fishing trips about 10:00 in the morning one can expect big rafts of floaters, and power boaters will start to show up, and some of them can be very noisy and disruptive. Go early, catch your fish, and get off the water when the yahoos show up.

Local Sources of Information

The Wilderness Way and its associated shuttle service T-n-T Hideaway (850-925-6412 or www.tnthideaway.com) are the best places to find specific up-to-the-moment information. Rob Baker, owner and operator of the two shops, knows the Wakulla very well—he grew up on the banks of the river, and he is a first class guide for anglers who want to really discover fishing on the Wakulla River.

Rob Baker knows the Wakulla River as well as anyone.
Here he plays a small Wakulla River bass.

Great Kayak Fishing Site 3

St. George Island, Franklin County, Florida

General Site Information

St. George is a big barrier island that lies off the coast of Florida near the mainland towns Apalachicola and East Point. The island is twenty-eight miles long from east to west, but it is only a couple miles across at its widest—most of the island is much narrower than that. St. George Island is a beautiful place with high white dunes, wind-beaten pine trees, lots of birds, lots of delicious local oysters, and lots of fish.

St. George Island brings the kayak angler from the mud and limestone rock bottom territory of the easternmost places we have visited and takes us into the white sand beaches and clear water of the Emerald Coast. But St. George Island is not like the frantic and often overcrowded parts of Florida; this island is definitely on "Island Time." From residents to visitors, folks just seem to slow down and take life easier on St. George. And it is a perfect place for kayak anglers to visit. There are lots of full time residents on the island and there are lots of rental beach houses, along with a few condos for visitors.

Kayak anglers can fish off the white sand beaches on the Gulf side when the surf allows safe launching, putting them into big game waters which hold king mackerel,

St. George Island has some wonderful white sand dunes to be explored.

cobia in season, massive redfish, most times of the year jack crevalle, and a host of other hard pullers.

When the surf is too high, or when the kayak angler just wants to fish bayou and backwater places, the north side of the island provides miles and miles of fine flats and oyster bars for some great inshore fishing. Reds, specks, flounder, and the usual list of inshore species are found all along the northern shore of St. George Island. There are many good launch spots for kayak anglers.

Probably the best place for kayak anglers to head is Dr. Julian G. Bruce/St. George Island State Park, which controls the eastern half of the island—it is a massive and gorgeous park with good roads and plenty of rest stops for showers and bathroom breaks. There are sixty campsites, including a more primitive campsite which can only be reached by hike or paddle.

But the best part of St. George State Park is East End. This totally wild and unsettled section of the island is the farthest part of the park away from the gate and from the crowds of folks who come to enjoy the beach. This part of the island is strictly controlled as far as how many people can enter it; you have to ask for access to East End at the ranger station, and if it is already full you are out of luck for the day. The road leading to the one parking area at East End is rough, and after a heavy rain it can be difficult to use for low vehicles, but when you get to the parking area and see the water that waits it is worth the long drive and bumpy road.

East End gives kayak anglers easy access to the pass between St. George Island and Dog Island to the east. The currents can be fierce at times, so exercise caution when paddling here. But the pass off East End is a grand place to find big reds, king mackerel in season, and cobia in season, and it is a very good place to find tarpon.

Obviously, this is not a fishing site for wimpy tackle or wimpy anglers. This location requires careful navigation and dependable gear. But even for folks who do not fish, East End is a beautiful place to just sit and watch the world go by.

Kayaks and redfish come together in the bayous of St. George Island.

How to Access the Area

This is pretty easy and pretty nice. The best way to reach St. George Island is to take old Hwy 98 and go west from the places we have already visited—St. Marks and the Wakulla River—and drive through the small coastal villages Panacea, Lanark, and Carrabelle; when you reach the town of Eastpoint—you'll know you are getting close when you see all of the oyster boats, oyster houses, and piles of oyster shells—you will turn south at the marked exit off Hwy 98 to St. George Island. This exit is right in the middle of Eastpoint. Go across the long bridge connecting the mainland and St. George Island and there is St. George Island ahead.

By the way, there are many, many good places to pull off Hwy 98 and slide the kayak in for a fishing trip as you travel from Wakulla River to St. George Island—this is a grand coast for kayak anglers.

Here is how those delicious Apalachicola Bay oysters get to the table. Tonging for oysters is hard work.

A Little Fish Story

It's July 5, and on the Gulf Coast that means this day is going to be hot-hot-hot. But that's just fine, because July 5, also means that tarpon will have made their annual migration from the lower parts of Florida—around the Keys mostly—and they will be back in Northern Gulf Coast waters, especially here around St. George Island. This big barrier island is a tarpon hotspot, and since the big silver fish can be found very close to the shoreline they are well within reach of kayak anglers. On both the southern Gulf side and the northern Apalachicola Bay side schools of big tarpon can be encountered. That does not mean they can be caught consistently. After all, we are talking about big, mature, more-than-one-hundred-pound tarpon. These are some powerful fish and hard to catch from any sort of craft, much less a kayak. But I am up for the challenge. At least, that is what I hope.

My wife and I slide our kayaks in at the East End of the island and I have my large level-wind reel with forty-lb. main line and fifty-lb. fluorocarbon leader on a stout, six-foot-long rod, and a suitably large circle hook. I have some fine mullet—tarpon candy—for bait. I think this rig will be heavy enough for me to have a chance of subduing a tarpon, but we will have to see. But I'm ready.

So we are going different directions and with very different purposes in mind on this fine, hot morning. My wife—who is not interested at all in catching a tarpon—has her typical twenty-lb. spinning rig and little small live shrimp. We had to buy the very last of the local bait shop's live shrimp, and these are truly shrimpy shrimp, to be sure. But because she wants to catch a nice flounder or redfish for supper she is taking the live bait bucket with the mini-shrimp.

Things start to happen quickly as we paddle off the beach. This is amazing. Tarpon are rolling everywhere around us. I see a tarpon—a real monster of a fish—roll up no more than ten feet behind my wife's little yellow kayak.

"What was that?" she yells to me.

"That was a tarpon," I yell back. "A big one—I want to catch him!"

So we fish. She lets the strong outgoing tide move her down the island as she bounces her shrimpy little two-inch-long shrimp along the bottom in search of supper. I am paddling my way toward where I can see several big, silver backs and sides rolling in the sun as they move along the white sand of the beach.

I have my delicious-looking mullet slowly trolling behind me—a very productive live bait fishing technique for hooking up with tarpon—but the only excitement I get is from

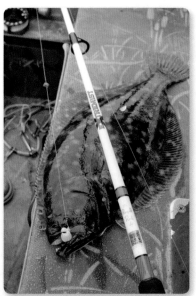

Flounder are common St. George Island catches. They look funny but taste great.

Use a kayak to quietly work St. George Island backwaters for some great speckled trout fishing.

Specks are gorgeous fish, and they are fine eating, too.

the big sea turtle that keeps popping up near me and my kayak and then making a crash dive below the surface.

A tarpon rolls close enough for me to spit on—what a magnificent looking fish—the only thing that would make it look better is if it were on the end of my line.

It is getting very hot and I am getting frustrated. Tarpon are everywhere around me but I can't get one to bite.

I hear a distant yell for me. My wife is paddling toward me, and I can tell from the way she is paddling that she is mad. I have been fishing with her many, many times before and I recognize the signs of anger.

As I go to meet her and see what's the trouble I hope that a tarpon will see my mullet speeding through the water and take it for a late breakfast—I'd like to show

Yes, we know where those summertime St. George Island tarpon are, and we will be back in the kayak for them.

my wife how the better sort of kayak angler hooks a tarpon. But no tarpon bites my mullet.

"I need a new rig," my wife says, and I can tell that she is not happy. "One of those big silver fish took my hook, sinker, and some line."

I stare at her, and then I say, "A tarpon broke you off?"

She gives me a look that means that I am wasting her valuable fishing time with dumb questions.

"Yes, a big silver fish broke my line and I need a new rig—now."

As I am re-rigging my wife's light rig I ask her, "Just what were you using for bait?"

Once again she gives me a look. She says, "I was using one of the little shrimps we got this morning. Hurry up so I can catch a redfish."

We part, me to try and fool a tarpon; they are still rolling all around us.

For another hour in the hot, hot sun I paddle around and slow-troll my delicious looking mullet, but no tarpon come to visit.

And then I hear my wife's call again.

She says, "I am out of shrimp and I'm tired of big fish breaking my line. Let's go get a shower and cool off."

"You hooked another tarpon?" I ask her quietly.

"Yes, and I'm tired of them taking my shrimp."

So we paddle back to the beach where our trusty old beach umbrella is casting a dark circle of shadow in the blinding light off the white sand.

I reel in my line and the mullet—that delicious, wonderfully tasty looking mullet—is still swimming well, still frisky, and happy to be alive. I unhook the mullet and it swims away perfectly pleased with the world after spending the morning swimming in the presence of totally uninterested tarpon.

But I know where the tarpon are and I will be back. Soon.

But next time I'm going to have a bucket of live shrimp. That's a promise.

Special Considerations

If you visit St. George in summer it is very likely you will stay on the beach, or at least near it. Please be aware that during turtle nesting season—the summer—all lights on houses and other sources are very strictly controlled and monitored. Baby sea turtles get confused by artificial lights and they sometimes do not make it to the water safely because of this. So when you stay here keep the lights off after dark.

Another special consideration when staying at St. George is that if you do not eat a lot of the world famous Apalachicola Bay oysters while you are here you will have missed a treat. Apalachicola oysters come from the waters of the bay just north of St. George Island, and these shellfish are wonderful cooked or raw. You'll very often see the fleet of small oyster boats as they work—and I do mean work—the different oyster beds around the bridge and other parts of Apalachicola Bay. The oysters you eat for supper were in the bay that morning. Kayak anglers could do a lot worse than spend a long day fishing and catching some fine St. George Island fish and then come in for a few rounds of oysters and cold beer.

Local Sources of Information

Kayak anglers who are interested in visiting St. George—and I highly recommend this island for a fishing trip—can get good helpful information about activities, housing, places to eat, and more from the St. George Island Visitor Center, 850-927-7754.

There are a number of kayak rental agencies on St. George Island. Journeys of St. George Island (850-927-3259 or www.stgeorgeislandjourneys.com) is a good one for folks who want to go fishing but who do not want to transport their own kayaks.

St. Joe Bay has some of the best kayak fishing for big specks found anywhere.

Great Kayak Fishing Site 4

St. Joe Bay, Gulf County, Florida

General Site Information

St. Joe Bay lies on the edge of the "Forgotten Coast" of northwest Florida. This large jewel of clear, protected water is near no large cities—the town of Port St. Joe is quite small, but it offers kayak anglers good places to eat and good places to stay.

The bay is fifteen miles long and about four miles or less wide.

The most impressive thing about St. Joe Bay—other than its clear, clean water—is the lush, healthy growth of various turtle grass beds over the bay's bottom. This grass helps filter the water and provides homes and protection to young fish, shrimp, and other marine life.

St. Joe Bay is open to the Gulf on its west end, allowing a wide range of fish species to enter the bay and spend time there.

Since there are no major feeder streams that empty into St. Joe Bay the water never gets cloudy or muddy from storm run-off and high water in upstream regions.

St. Joe Bay offers at least three first rate launch areas and docks for powerboats, but for kayak anglers, the bay is open for "park the car, unload the kayak, and go fishing" situations. Much of the bay's shoreline is readily accessible to kayak anglers. As long as kayak anglers do not cross private property they can launch their kayaks freely.

The east end of the bay—that's the end that CR 30A runs parallel with—is quite shallow, so kayakers will often have to wade their kayaks out for a quarter of a mile or more to reach water deep enough to paddle or pedal their kayaks.

Kayak anglers who drive out on the Cape San Blas Peninsula on CR 30E will see a big line of massive boulders that protects the roadway from the heavy surf conditions of the Gulf. On the other side of CR 30E at this boulder section of road is a launch area specifically dedicated to kayakers. This nice launch area has good parking, and it takes only a few minute's paddle to put kayak anglers in some very good fishing water.

T. H. Stone State Park lies on the Cape San Blas Peninsula across the bay from the town of Port St. Joe; this park is one of the best public parks to be found anywhere. There is a fine boat ramp and beach area for kayak launches, and some great grass beds lie right out from the park's marina. There is good close parking for kayak anglers, too. If planning to stay at the park for camping—and that's a very good idea—make reservations well in advance. This is a very popular and heavily used park area, especially during the summer scalloping season.

Kayak anglers can find good protection for windy conditions by choosing sides of the bay to access: if the wind is from the south go to the Cape San Blas Peninsula. If the wind is from the north launch from the Port St. Joe side. If the wind is from the east launch from the shallow eastern side.

There are a couple islands which lie in the bay off the eastern shore, and these islands—Black's Island is the larger one with large private homes built on it, and Bird Island (much smaller and settled only by many nesting seabirds)—are both very good places for kayak anglers to paddle to and fish around.

To say that St. Joe Bay is a good kayak fishing destination is an understatement. This is a wonderful place to visit and spend some time fishing from a kayak.

Kayak anglers can fish the deeper open waters of St. Joe Bay for a wide range of large game fish. Spanish mackerel, bull redfish, very large speckled trout, big jack crevalle, and even tarpon will be found during the warm months. There are also some very large sharks in St. Joe Bay—lots of them.

Fishing the shallow waters of the bay is a pleasure. Most of the time, depending on light conditions, kayak anglers can have a ball sight fishing for slot-size redfish and trout. A special feature of the bay is the presence of "potholes" on its eastern end. These potholes are sandy depressions; they show up very clearly as light-colored, roughly circular or elongated patches of sandy bottom. In contrast to the dark grass beds, the potholes offer a clear background for anglers to see fish and cast to them.

St. Joe Bay is a world class location for kayak anglers to hook and fight some big redfish and trout on topwater lures. A large walk-the-dog-type lure works well. Just throw the lure as far as possible—long casts are necessary here, with the super-clear water of the bay allowing the fish to see anglers from a distance. Then slowly work the lure back in. When a mega-red or gator trout explodes on the lure there will be no doubt about it. Expect to see lures bounced into the air, thrown across the surface, and sometimes just completely sucked down in to a fish's gullet. This is a very, very exciting brand of topwater fishing, and kayak anglers will be in a position to experience it at its best.

And why is it called "Bird Island?" There is some great fishing for kayakers on the shallow flats around this island.

Kayak anglers at St. Joe Bay can expect to find some very good specks.

St. Joe Bay is a wonderful place for fly rod anglers, too. Kayak anglers who have kayaks which allow them to stand and fish are in prime position to experience some great fly fishing. It takes long casts, but when the wind is light this is quite possible. Fly rodders will want to use at least 8 wt. rods here—the fish can be large. Large poppers and gurglers work very well; I like a white crease fly. Clousers and other streamers in white and silver flash will attract a lot of attention. Fly rodders can expect to encounter some aggressive fish here.

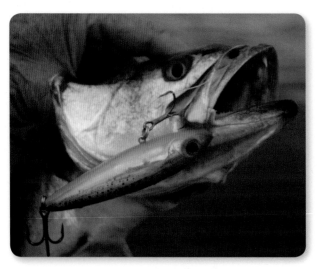

Work a topwater plug over grass flats at St. Joe Bay and hang on.

In the open waters of St. Joe Bay some massive jack crevalle can be encountered, and when they are found the fight for kayak anglers will not be short.

It is also very possible and often very productive for kayak anglers to bail out of their kayak over a shallow bar and wade fish. Either tie the kayak to yourself or *securely* anchor or stake the boat. It is discouraging to wade fish a good bar and then turn around to see your kayak floating merrily away without you.

Also, when wading St. Joe Bay shuffle your feet as you move. There are very many stingrays here, and although they will not seek out or attack a wader, they will sting anyone who steps on them. I have been zapped by a stingray, and I assure you, good readers, it is not something you want to experience, so do the stingray shuffle as you wade along.

For the ultimate in kayak fishing adventure, hook up with one of the many large sharks that live in St. Joe Bay and go for a kayak sleigh ride. It is not hard to find and hook a shark. Just throw out a pinfish or other smaller non-keeper fish on a large, strong hook secured to a steel leader and let it drift behind your kayak as you fish.

Make sure the rod is in a secure rod holder and do not just hang it over the side of the 'yak—that is the best way I know to lose a fishing rod here. When a shark takes the bait the kayak will follow. Just hold on, let the big shark run, and enjoy the ride. If the shark is too big—and that decision is up to the angler—just cut the line and let the shark go. The hook will soon rust and fall away with no harm to the shark.

Do not bring a shark of any size into your kayak. This is important. Sharks, even quite small ones, can deliver vicious and potentially quite serious bites to anglers.

When out of the kayak and wade fishing St. Joe Bay shuffle your feet to avoid stepping on a stingray.

Sharks get big in St. Joe Bay. Do not try to land a shark of any size from a kayak.

When the shark is whipped down and tired out get it to the side of the kayak, and using the line lift the fish's head high enough for some photos, then use pliers to cut the leader at least a foot away from the shark's mouth. Wish the shark well and watch it swim off.

How to Access the Area

From I-10, exit at Marianna and head south on Hwy 71. Stay on 71 for about seventy miles through the small towns Altha, Blountstown, and the fascinating Dead Lakes at Wewahitchka. Highway 71 will lead directly into the town Port St. Joe.

Please watch your speed as you head south on Hwy 71, especially when it enters small towns and settlements. This road is patrolled heavily for speeders. (See the earlier sidebar for an alternative and even more attractive route to St. Joe Bay from Wakulla River on old Hwy 98—it is a great ride.)

A Little Fish Story

The sun was not nearly up over the trees, so the water on the east end of St. Joe Bay was still quite shaded. The eagle who lives with his mate here was sitting up in his dead pine tree on the small island; he seemed more interested in watching me fish than going fishing himself.

The resident St. Joe Bay bald eagles let kayak anglers approach closely. These are very impressive birds.

Mullet jumped. A few cars drove past on County Road 30-A. It was a fine, fine morning. But I was here to fight.

I cast my yellow and silver topwater plug as far as I could out over the grass beds. I let the impact rings spread out and fade, then I started a slow retrieve. The quiet and peace of this gorgeous morning made me grateful to be here in my old wooden kayak fishing this clear, pristine water.

And then that magic moment came. I saw the water bulge about ten feet away from my plug and then a wake approached with a definite purpose in mind.

When that redfish hit my plug it was like a small detonation. A massive strike, and this time, unlike many topwater strikes from reds, the fish actually got the lure and got hooked.

My reel made funny noises and the redfish made some long, strong runs out toward deeper water. I have always loved catching redfish, and this particular red was giving me a real struggle. In the clear St. Joe Bay water I could see the bronze sides of the redfish flash as it fought against the pressure of my line. All reds are strong fish, but this red seemed to be particularly stout and determined not to come in to me.

And then the fish went crazy. This redfish—he was about ten pounds or so—started making short, frantic runs with quick changes in direction, I had never had a redfish act this way before and I wondered what was going on.'

But then, I had never hooked a redfish that had a six-foot-long shark after it before either. The shark made the same wake as it ran toward my hooked redfish that the redfish did when it attacked my plug—and the shark wanted to do to the red what the red had done to my lure.

In a case like this there is only one thing to do: let line run free and hope the hooked fish can escape the shark, so I flipped the bail of my reel open and just gave slack line. On cue the redfish ran and ran and ran, and the shark was soon left behind,

There are lots of fine redfish in St. Joe Bay for kayak anglers. There will be a good fight from a redfish no matter what size it is.

I fully expected the redfish would be long gone—that's what usually happens when a big fish gets slack line. But when I took up slack the red was still hooked up, though he was a long way out there away from me.

I started to work the red back to my boat and he made a little bit of resistance, but I think he was tired from his close escape.

When I got the nice red back to kayak side I was able to gently lift it from the water, and using the pliers I always have on the kayak with me I was able to remove the treble hooks from the big red's jaws.

I lowered the fish back into the clear water of the bay and it slowly finned beside the kayak for a little while; then, when it decided it was time to leave, it showered me with a splash of water—which in case you don't know it is the fish's blessing, giving thanks to the angler who let it go.

I felt blessed this morning.

Special Considerations

During scallop season, which occurs most summers during June and July through early fall, St. Joe Bay is a very popular place. It can be very difficult to find housing at this time unless long-previous reservations have been made. The state campground will be packed full, too. Kayak anglers will still be able to access the water and fishing will still be good, but there will be lots of scallopers on the water during the middle of the day. Of course, there is no reason kayak anglers can't be scallop

Here is what a delicious St. Joe Bay scallop looks like on the hoof. Kayak anglers can have good scalloping during the summer season.

divers, too, and snorkeling for scallops is a really fun thing to do—and the scallops are delicious.

For visiting kayak anglers, when it comes time to find some place to eat, Sunset Grill in Port St. Joe is a very good restaurant; I recommend their grilled tuna very much. Also out on 30-A, past the state park turn-off, is the famous Indian Pass Raw Bar—an oyster bar of considerable fame. Expect long waits for supper, but it is much easier to get in for a table at lunch. You will probably admire the "wall of beer" featured at the Raw Bar, along with the excellent local oysters.

On another less happy note, at times bugs can be bad around the shorelines of St. Joe Bay so have bug spray and protective garments.

Local Sources of Information
There are two good bait and tackle shops in Port St. Joe that can help kayak anglers with advice, lure selections, and live bait. Half-Hitch Bait and Tackle (psj@halfhitch.com or 850-227-7100) is right on the main road in Port St. Joe, and Bluewater Outriggers (850-229-1100 or www.bluewateroutriggers.com) is in the one small shopping center at the stoplight in downtown Port St. Joe.

St. Joe Bay has beautiful shorelines and clear, clean water perfect for kayak anglers.

Great Kayak Fishing Site 5
Navarre Beach, Escambia County, Florida

General Site Information

Here is another place that I can't be totally objective about. Navarre Beach has the nicest water and the best beaches of the entire Gulf Coast, bar none. It also has some world-class kayak fishing.

Even though the Navarre Beach area has excellent inshore fishing for reds and specks in the waters of Santa Rosa Sound, which separates the island from the mainland, we are going to focus on the fishing that happens once a kayak angler leaves the sugar-white beach and paddles out into the open Gulf.

Simply put, Navarre Beach is the best place on the entire Gulf Coast for kayak anglers to encounter some very big fish that are usually associated with either far offshore or more exotic—and very expensive—fishing locations. Kayak anglers here hook and catch very large king mackerel, bull redfish, mahi-mahi (dolphin fish), cobia, and even tuna and sailfish. The deep blue water of the Gulf curves closer to land at Navarre than just about anywhere else on the entire Gulf coastline, bringing the big pelagic game fish within reach. Kayak anglers who paddle no more than five miles offshore can reach some great bottom structure and fight with some very big red snapper.

Sunrise at Navarre Beach; big water gives kayak anglers a totally different kind of fishing experience.

Getting the kayak to the water from the parking area across the white, soft sand can be tough, but the fishing is worth the effort.

There is even a major project underway to construct a large system of artificial reefs just offshore along the coast at Navarre, so the open Gulf big game fishing for kayak anglers stands to get even better. Truly, Navarre Beach should be on the radar for any kayak angler who is serious about fishing beyond the breakers.

Kayak anglers may not need to get a bigger boat, but they may need to obtain bigger tackle for the offshore fishing at Navarre Beach. Before heading off the beach kayak anglers will need to have a rig or two holding at least 250 yards of twenty-five-lb. line—either mono or braid. Both heavy spinning rigs and level wind rigs will work, but whichever rig is selected, the drag of the reel must be smooth and easy to adjust. This is not idle talk—there are big fish just offshore at Navarre Beach and shoddy equipment will not work here.

The best thing about big game fishing from a kayak at Navarre is that the angler won't have to paddle far. Many big fish are hooked and caught within a half-mile of the beach. Kayak anglers need to launch, paddle out past the breakers, and when the water changes color—gets darker—start fishing.

The best bait for big game fishing here is live bait. Kayak anglers can use a sabiki rig—these can be purchased at any local bait and tackle shop—to catch the smaller fish that are the natural food for the big fish. Frozen cigar minnows and Spanish sardines work well, too. A wire double-hook stinger rig—also available at local bait and tackle shops—completes the rig. Hook up the bait, cast it behind your kayak, and just slowly paddle or pedal along. Either put the rod in a very secure rod holder or keep it in hand with a very good grip. When the strike comes it will usually be shockingly

There are lots of good parking areas along the beach road at Navarre Beach.

strong. Have the drag set light and let the hooked fish run. This is not the time to get excited and try to rush the fish. You can't catch a big fish at this point, but you sure can lose one if you try to do too much.

Then have a good time fighting your fish back to the boat and don't be surprised if you get taken for a kayak sleigh ride.

How to Access the Area

From I-10, turn south at the Milton exit and drive about twenty miles on Hwy 87. When Hwy 87 ends you are at Navarre. Turn left at the stoplight and go perhaps a mile until the Navarre Beach Bridge appears. Turn right at the stop light and cross the bridge— paradise lies just ahead.

Once on the island at Navarre Beach kayak anglers can turn right on the main beach road; the road will parallel the beach all the way to Pensacola Beach (about twenty miles). Kayak anglers can use any of the pull-off parking areas.

Here is a favorite bait for open gulf fishing: cigar minnows either caught alive or bought frozen work very well.

Those teeth are just as sharp as they look. Keep fingers and toes clear of big king mackerel.

Hooking a big king mackerel is a world-class thrill for kayak anglers.

A word of warning: when kayak fishing the Navarre Beach waters, it is perfectly acceptable to launch your kayak off the beach near the long fishing pier, but do not hug the pier either going out or coming back in to the beach. The pier anglers take great exception to kayakers—or any other boaters—who come within casting distance of the pier. Stay at least one hundred yards away from the pier—200 yards is better.

A Little Fish Story

It is just the purest morning. The night is leaving and the eastern horizon is glowing with the coming day. The surf is low—almost none at all—and I have dragged my kayak from the parking lot to the water, so I'm winded. Even with a soft-tired beach cart to help move the 'yak, this soft powdery Navarre Beach sand makes transport of a kayak hard . . . In many ways, this is the hardest part of the whole expedition, getting the kayak from the truck to the water.

But now I wade the kayak out into knee deep water, hop in, and paddle off the beach area. I drop the pedal drive unit into place, and in just a few minutes of easy pedaling I am out past the second bar and over deeper, darker, more dangerous water. The clear Gulf water is alive with schools of bait fish darting nervously as the shadow of my kayak crosses over them. I expect the poor little fish have plenty to be nervous about—this is king mackerel water after all.

Kings are strong and very fast. Have the reel's drag set light and let the hooked fish run and pull the kayak.

I am using frozen cigar minnows as bait—not as good as fresh live bait, but easy to obtain, and the big kings usually like a frozen bait-cicle for a snack. I hook up a frozen cig, cast it out, and start a slow troll about 200 yards off the beach.

I admire the clear water. I admire the sun starting to peek over the horizon and the color change in the water as the day grows older. I admire the quiet and peace of the scene, and then . . . My rod in the holder bends over violently and then my reel makes a noise like a thing in pain. Line rips off my reel as something very big and very fast heads for the deep blue water far offshore.

At times like this all I can do is just hang on and see what develops. After a ten-second run that seems to last a week the big fish slows, the run stops, and I am able to tighten the drag just a little and start my steady pressure retrieve.

I work the big fish back, and about forty yards out it decides that this course of events is not to its liking and another lightning fast run occurs. Again line is torn from my reel, and again my reel makes that strange noise.

I work carefully to move the fish closer to the kayak. The hooked fish has pulled me a ways offshore in its runs, but now I think I am starting to win the fight.

I get the fish close enough to my kayak that I can see it in the clear water. As I thought, this is a very, very nice king mackerel—well over twenty pounds.

I know what is coming next. This is the point in the fight when big fish get away. I make sure my drag is loose enough, because at this point big kings almost always make one last final-effort run, and this is when hooks pull, lines break, and fish get away.

Sure enough one last smoking run comes, and when this run stops I know I have this battle won—mostly.

I work the big king to my kayak and it makes a couple circles around the boat, pulling with its last strength against my line. When I have the big fish quiet by the kayak I admire its form—about four feet of steel-colored power with a big sickle-shaped tail on one end and a big mouth full of daggers for teeth at the other.

Launching off the beach goes better with a friend on hand to help keep things straight.

A double kayak hook-up—these Navarre Beach kings can be very aggressive.

On calm days everyone can go kayak fishing at Navarre Beach.

I grab my long-nosed pliers—required equipment for this kind of fishing; I am not getting my fingers close to those extremely sharp teeth—and I carefully twist free the stinger hook that has done its job so well.

As the hook pulls free the big king slowly sinks into the water, and I have the pleasure of seeing it give one pump with its massive tail, another pump, and then the big silver lightning bolt is gone.

Now what do I do with the rest of this morning's trip?

Special Considerations

Any time kayak anglers launch off the beach and into the Gulf care must be taken during launch and landing procedures. Safe kayak launching in a surf is a difficult skill, and lots of gear is lost to anglers who let the surf get their kayaks sideways and then rolled over.

It would be best for most kayak anglers who are not familiar with beach launching to go with a guide or an experienced beach kayak angler first. The main point is simple: keep the sharp end of the kayak—either bow or stern—pointed into the waves and you will probably be all right. Let the boat get sideways and bad things happen very fast.

If there is much surf—to me this means much over knee high—it may not be a good off-the-beach fishing day. Also, keep in mind that surf does not stay the same, and a day which started with dead flat no surf conditions can have bad breaking, dangerous surf in just a few hours.

Along the twenty-mile run of the beach road between Navarre Beach and Pensacola Beach there are several good launch spots. Please do not cross private property to reach the beach. Use public access areas and be sure to park in designated parking areas. Parking on the shoulder of the road is very tempting sometimes, but it will result in a towed vechicle.

Local Sources of Information

Matthew Vann (850-572-6563, www.sailsandtailskayakcharters.com) is a local kayak angler who takes visitors and locals alike fishing from the Navarre beaches, and he is a very good person to speak with concerning kayak fishing trips here. He is a good man to learn the skills and techniques of this specialized kind of fishing from.

Pensacola Fishing Forum is a great online local fishing information source; there is a whole section of the forum devoted to kayak anglers and their reports and questions. This is a great place to start gathering information for a planned trip.

Broxson Outdoors (850-936-0230) is a first-class bait and tackle shop specializing in getting anglers prepared for the Navarre Beach area—and they have an extensive kayak fishing section. They carry live and frozen bait. Broxson Outdoors is on Hhwy 98, about two miles west of the Navarre Beach Bridge.

Great Kayak Fishing Site 6
Pensacola Bay, Escambia County, Florida

General Site Information

Pensacola Bay is a massive body of water, stretching for more than thirteen miles from north of the I-10 bridge down to the pass where the bay empties into the Gulf at Fort Pickens National Park. There is a very wide range of possible kayak fishing venues here, from shallow water casting for reds and specks to fishing deep water structure for bull reds, grouper, and even red snapper. During the summer some monstrous king mackerel are caught in Pensacola Bay as they cruise the waters looking for easy prey. All of these fisheries are possible—in the right conditions—for kayak anglers.

One of the best and most reliable fisheries in Pensacola Bay is the big redfishing that is done by kayakers around the Three Mile Bridge crossing from Pensacola to Gulf Breeze. This bridge has good launch areas at both ends, and kayak anglers can fish around the bridge structure for some very big redfish all year long, sheepshead in season, and at night, during the summer, there is a very good tarpon fishery under the bridge lights.

Kayak anglers can launch from many areas on the upper reaches of the bay, and with caution can launch and fish the pass area. The pass demands a lot of skill and respect for the water. The current at the pass can be quite strong, and combined with boat wakes can be quite rough. But the fishing can be very good there, too.

During late fall and winter massive schools of very big redfish form in the bay, and in the pass and the beach area just outside Pensacola Pass. These reds feed heavily on pogies and other bait fish which move from the bay out into the Gulf for winter. If a kayak angler can find a school of big reds and get close enough to make a cast, an immediate hook up with a very big, very strong fish is assured.

Quite often these big schools of large reds can be seen just off the beaches and in the bay, but they tend to move quickly and can be difficult to follow in a kayak. If a school shows up and decides to stay in a particular area for a while some truly amazing fishing from a kayak can and does happen.

Gag grouper can be caught by kayak anglers who work deeper structure in the bay.

Flounder will be found on sandy bottoms near drop-offs.

Several long bridges on Pensacola Bay and nearby waters give kayak anglers lots of good fishing.

For this bull redfish in the pass and off the beach fishery, kayak anglers can get lots of help locating feeding reds by watching birds; look for flocks of diving, screaming birds as they dip and crash into the water. Most of the time the big reds will be below the birds.

How to Access the Area

From I-10, exit on I-110 and continue on I-110 south and east. This will take you through downtown Pensacola—not a big deal usually—and then I-110 will intersect at the water with Bayfront Drive. Pensacola Bay lies dead ahead.

Anglers can launch kayaks from the launch area or even from the parking area on the Pensacola side. On the Gulf Breeze side kayakers can use the ramps or just lift and carry to the water.

A Little Fish Story

Whap-whap, whap-whap. That is the sound of tires hitting the expansion joint of the Pensacola Bay Bridge which looms above me. Lots of people are driving over me on their way to work, and I am going fishing.

I launched my kayak at the Pensacola end of the bridge and pedaled out along the massive bridge pilings until I reached the place I wanted to stop. My bucket of live shrimp was stowed and riding well, so I was set for some good action.

The Three Mile Bridge over Pensacola Bay is a very reliable fish producer for kayak anglers, with good access at both ends of the bridge.

There was the familiar old nylon line someone had looped around one of the big concrete pillars which support the bridge and traffic above. I grabbed the helpful line, made my own bow line secure, and let the easy current take me back under the bridge and into the shade.

Now this is nice. No pedaling required and comfortable shade. Only one thing more is needed—some agreeable fish.

I had a medium-heavy spinning rig with me on this trip because I had been taken to school on my last trip to the Bay Bridge; big fish just overpowered my usual gear I like to use on slot size reds and trout. On that earlier trip much bigger bull reds broke me off immediately or just stripped the line off my reel and then broke me off. I came better prepared today with heavier gear.

So a nice lively shrimp on a circle hook with a half-ounce sliding sinker above the leader swivel was tossed a short distance to the side of the next piling of the bridge, and there was an immediate and sharp strike, a good pull, and then nothing. Fish got a meal—I got taken.

That's fine—you never want to catch a fish on the first cast—bad luck, don't you know.

So I baited up again, tossed back, and let the shrimp sink into the dark water. It truly was nice fishing here at ease in the coolness of the bridge's shadow.

Whap-whap. Whap-whap.

Above me on the roadway a heavy flow of traffic over the bridge let me know that the regular world was going on; folks were going to work and taking care of the world.

I was certainly glad I did not have to commute to work on this day. I was very happy to be where I was. And I got happier in just a second.

My rod bent over, my reel screeched a bit, and I had a fine ten-pound redfish on my line giving me a very good fight. This fish pulled for a while, then I got it to the kayak where I could admire it and let it go.

This pattern was a good one, and it repeated a number of times. I never had to move at all—the fish just liked this place. While I fished, the traffic went on and on above me. I am happy to stay in one spot and catch redfish for as long as these wonderful fish want to bite—and these reds seemed willing to bite all morning.

Then I got a very sharp bite, and this fish acted differently from the reds I had been catching. This fish was fast; it changed directions very quickly, unlike the straight-ahead pulls of the reds. No doubt about it, this was a different kind of fish.

I got this mysterious stranger of a fish closer to my kayak and I could see silver sides flashing in the water, and then I got excited. I thought I had a state record pompano hooked. Same round shape, same strong, fast pull, same blunt, rounded nose.

Big bull redfish will be found around Pensacola Bay bridges year round.

A permit! These hard fighters are not especially common in Pensacola Bay, but they do show up from time to time.

But when I got the fish to the surface and safely landed in the kayak I was shocked. This was no pompano. Look: there's a black splotch on the broad side. There's a bright orange-yellow belly to this fish. This is a permit! People spend lots and lots of money to travel to the Keys and other exotic places to catch permit, and these permit specialists obsess over the power and difficulty in hooking and catching these wonderful fish. And here I was catching one under the Three Mile Bridge at Pensacola.

Now, being only six or seven pounds, this juvie permit would not get much comment in the Florida Keys or other places where it grows to massive sizes and is such a highly sought after fish, but here—this is a pretty nice fish.

And that is the joy of kayak fishing the Pensacola Bay, especially the Pensacola Bay Bridge. You never know what kind of fishy opponent is going to show up. Lots of reds, lots of specks, lots of flounder, and lots of tarpon in the summer. And even the occasional permit.

Whap whap. Whap whap.

Special Considerations

Pensacola Bay is big water and it deserves respect. Tidal currents can be strong, and a south or north wind can kick up some prodigious seas remarkably quickly. Kayakers need to watch the weather and be ready to make a fast retreat to shore if the weather starts to fall apart.

Many kayak anglers launch at Fort Pickens and fish the pass, as this can be very productive. Again, keep an eye on weather and water conditions because they can change quickly here. There is almost always some kind of tidal movement at the pass, and it can get very rough when an outgoing tide meets an incoming swell from the Gulf.

On another note, one very cool thing about fishing the pass area is that Pensacola Naval Air Station is right across the bay from Fort Pickens, and the Navy's flight demonstration team the Blue Angels is based there. All during the summer the Blues put on practice shows during the middle of the week and kayak anglers can find some great fishing while watching some world-class flying.

Redfish of all sizes give Pensacola Bay kayak anglers lots of fast action.

King mackerel are often caught by kayak anglers on Pensacola Bay in the warm months.

When kayak fishing under the bridge make sure that other boaters can see you: have lights at night and a warning flag during the day. Lots of boats travel the waters around the Bay Bridge and kayaks can be hard to see when they are among the bridge structure.

Local Sources of Information

Pensacola Fishing Forum is a first rate online source covering all of the fishing in the Pensacola area. It has a specific forum for kayak anglers and these are some very knowledgeable folks.

Sails and Tails Kayak Charters is a good local guide service for the Pensacola area (850-572-6563 or sailsandtailskayakcharters.com).

There is a good bait and tackle shop—Gulf Breeze Bait and Tackle—just across the bridge from Pensacola where anglers can get live bait and information (www. gbbtonline.com or 850-932-6789).

Visit Pensacola (800-874-1234, www.pensacola.org) is the official tourism and visitor help desk.

A kayak and a redfish—a perfect and common Pensacola Bay arrangement.

Notes

ALABAMA

Not what you expected from Alabama? Some great coastal and offshore fishing waters can be found in 'Bama.

Kayak anglers from out of the Gulf Coast region might look at the short run of coastline that Alabama possesses and decide this state's coastal fishing could be skipped. What a mistake that would be.

Even though Alabama only has forty miles or so of straightline coast, there are many, many miles of associated great fishing water for kayak anglers. Lots of bays, bayous, creeks, big Gulf passes, and fresh water feeder streams provide kayak anglers in coastal Alabama a lifetime of fishing choices.

Some very good kayak shops in Alabama make any needed kayak repairs or equipment purchases quick and easy, too.

Most, if not all, of Alabama's coastal kayak fishing waters have free public access, and the entire coastal area of Alabama is very kayak friendly.

Shrimp boats and bayous—wonderful backwater kayak fishing is all along the Alabama coast.

Using I-10 as the primary entry, kayak anglers can quickly get to salt water for some big fish action. In fact, I-10 crosses Mobile Bay, and kayak anglers are only moments away from some fine fishing—sometimes right under the I-10 elevated roadway.

Kayak anglers can exit I-10 at the Loxley exit, drop down on Highway 59, and be at the white sand beaches of Orange Beach and Gulf Shores in less than an hour. On the west side of the bay kayak anglers can make the short forty-five-minute run to Dauphin Island and other fishing spots on Mobile Bay and the Mississippi Sound with little trouble.

There are lots of bait and tackle shops in the Alabama Gulf Coast area and these are usually the best sources of local information.

Another very good source of Alabama coastal fishing advice is the Mobile Bay Kayak Fishing Association: an online group of avid kayak anglers who provide lots of specific and up-to-the-minute reports and advice for kayak anglers—they're good folks.

What Kinds of Kayak Fishing

There is something for everyone when it comes to kayak fishing on the Alabama Gulf Coast. Anglers can put 'yaks in far up the Mobile-Tensaw Delta and catch all kinds of freshwater fish—the bass fishing in particular is very good, and the spring crappie fishing around cypress trees and fallen wood in the water up in the Mobile Delta can be phenomenal. Fishing with worms or crickets around the many cypress trees of the Delta can produce a big stringer of delicious bream of all kinds.

Mobile Bay offers a wide range of saltwater fishing. Redfish, speckled trout, flounder, black drum, sheepshead, big crevalle jacks—these are commonly encountered on the bay from the I-10 bridge all the way to the gulf.

Take the kayak upstream to fresh water and find some great bass fishing.

If anglers choose to spend their Alabama fishing time down on the white sand beach areas a wide range of saltwater species are commonly found, including mackerel—both king and Spanish—extra large redfish, sharks, and even tarpon during the warm weather season. When the warm water fish leave for winter big schools of massive redfish take over the inshore coastal waters—they are prime kayak fishing targets and lots of fun to hook and play with.

In short, if it swims in warm water it is probably found in coastal Alabama for kayak anglers to catch—or try to.

The Mobile-Tensaw Delta gives kayak anglers a world of fishing choices.

Sunrise over coastal Alabama; another great day fishing for kayak anglers.

Housing and Food for Visitors

Kayak anglers who visit the Alabama coast will have no problem locating housing; from low budget motels to upscale beach mansion rentals, it is all here.

Some great state parks give kayak anglers who prefer camping some good choices, too. Meaher Park is right off the I-10 exit at Spanish Fort. Gulf Shores State Park, down at the beach, is a wonderful park with cabins for rent, RV camping, and tent camping—just be sure and call ahead for reservations; do not assume a place will be open, especially during the busy summer season. Dauphin Island, on the west side of Mobile Bay, has a fine camping park and lots of rental housing, too. Again, make reservations and call ahead of time if you plan to be here on the coast, especially during peak summer season.

There are many great seafood restaurants in lower Alabama for visiting kayak anglers to enjoy, but the easiest place to find great seafood is right along the causeway off I-10: The Bluegill, Original Oyster House, Ed's Seafood Shed, and Felix's Fish Camp—these are long-time businesses and established eating places, and they serve up some great food. And they don't mind serving kayak anglers just off the water, either.

Other Things to Do

For kayak anglers do not want to spend their entire lives fishing—or perhaps for family members who don't fish—there are loads of non-fishing things to do.

Just off I-10, on the Mobile side of the bay, is the Battleship *Alabama* Memorial Park—a great place to take kids to show them a bit of history in a very interesting setting.

Mobile, Alabama, is the original home of Mardi Gras, and every small town along the coast has its own Mardi Gras parade.

For visiting kayak anglers, a side trip to a Mardi Gras parade is a great way to enjoy coastal Alabama.

In Mobile there are a number of parks and historical displays which show the early history of Mobile—it is an old, old place.

Just taking the kids to any of the white sand beaches along the Alabama coast is fun and the beach fishing is quite good, too.

Of course, if a kayak angler decides to come to the coast during Mardi Gras season—it varies time from year to year—Mobile has some large and impressive parades. After all, Mardi Gras began in Mobile, not that other old city to the west in Louisiana. Most of the smaller towns on the coast have their own Mardi Gras parades and celebrations, too. I particularly recommend the Mardi Gras parades at Dauphin Island—family-friendly and not too rowdy at all. It is a lot of fun for everyone to watch the parade and yell for someone to, "throw me something, Mister!"

On the eastern side of the bay there are many amusement parks at the end of Hwy 59 at Gulf Shores and Orange Beach that kids love, as well as a very good zoo.

For those who like shopping there is a massive Tanger Outlet Mall at Foley on Hwy 59, where non-anglers can spend many hours shopping—I much prefer fishing.

Mobile Bay is a massive body of water full of big fish for kayak anglers to catch.

Great Kayak Fishing Site 7
Wolf Creek/Wolf Bay, Baldwin County, Alabama

General Site Information

For kayak anglers, Wolf Creek starts as a rather small stream up at the very nice county-operated kayak launch just off CR 20 in southern Baldwin County. Anglers at this point can paddle downstream and fish for saltwater fish—reds, specks, flounder, and such—or paddle upstream and fish for saltwater fish and freshwater fish, like bass and bream.

Kayak anglers won't go far wrong using live shrimp under a cork here, but soft plastic grubs on ¼ oz. jigheads also work very well, especially on trout in the cooler months.

Kayak anglers can paddle downstream a couple miles, and the creek opens wide into Wolf Bay, which is a fairly shallow and open bay with plenty of private residences on the shoreline, and these residences all have boat docks and private piers. These man-made structures, especially the ones with all-night lights, offer kayak anglers some of the best nighttime fishing around. Lots of specks gather under the lights in summer and fall when they eat the shrimp and small fish that are attracted to the lights, and the big reds will be under the trout, unless the big reds decide to eat stuff on top.

Even though Wolf Creek is not far from the heavy tourism development of Foley and Orange Beach, it is still a pretty wild place with lots of shore birds, ospreys, and

Sunrise over Wolf Creek and boat docks that attract fish—prime kayak fishing locations.

Kayak anglers on Wolf Creek often find some great redfish action.

The kayak launch at upper Wolf Creek gives kayak anglers a wonderful access point— we need more of this kind of facility.

Specks can be thick in the open water of Wolf Creek and upper Wolf Bay.

even a pair or two of nesting eagles. Porpoises come far up the creek at times.

The best thing about Wolf Creek is the excellent county-made kayak launch area. This area has great shaded parking, and the parking is very close to the dock, with its inclined slide for launching kayaks. From the launch to the creek is perhaps fifty yards.

Wolf Creek is a fine place for kayak anglers.

How to Access the Area

From I-10, exit on Hwy 59 south at the Loxley exit. Keep south on Hwy 59 through Loxley, Robertsdale, and into Foley. In Foley, turn left on to Baldwin Co. Road 20—this turn is at Lambert's Restaurant, a good place to eat after a kayak trip. Stay on CR 20 east. You will cross Sandy Creek and Wolf Creek on CR 20. Turn right on Wilson Road. Stay on Wilson Road and then turn on Hance Lane—this will lead to the kayak launch.

Hwy 59 can be very busy on the weekends when tourists turn around for their vacation weeks at the beach, and there is a big shopping mall on Hwy 59 to complicate things. Middle of the week trips and very early and late trips are best.

A Little Fish Story

The days are getting shorter, and the nights— well, they are getting darker. But this can only be expected—it's fall, getting toward winter, and even here on the Gulf Coast things are changing to the winter way of life.

The first cool front has come through, and lots of things are on the move from their shallow water homes in the swamps and bayous where they found lots of nutrition during the warm months; now shrimp and small fish are moving out of the shallow waters into deeper, warmer places where they will winter over.

But getting to these winter homes for the small fry is difficult. Lots of big, hungry

Here's what we want! Topwater fishing for reds is just about the best kind of kayak fishing fun.

things that love to eat shrimp and small fish are just waiting for a chance to end their travels quickly.

I paddled my kayak through the still, very early morning darkness from the launch at Old Wolf Bay Lodge upstream, and I hoped my early morning trip was going to be worth the trouble. I do not really enjoy paddling in the dark, but sometimes a dark-thirty kayak trip is worth the extra effort and diligence required. I approached the goal of my trip, a special lighted boat dock which generally holds good fish. I let my kayak drift very quietly toward the destination and got ready for fishing.

Here under the lights of the dock on the upper reaches of Wolf Bay there is a cloud of shrimp and small pogies and other bait fish clustered around the lights. All night in the darkness these lights have attracted plankton and other tiny critters, and the shrimp and bait fish have gathered to feed on the plankton.

And every so often the water under the glow of the dock lights erupts as something much, much bigger explodes into the small fry.

I have found that some dock lights, for whatever reason, are just better than others, and the one I am fishing this early morning is a prime dock light. Actually there are three dock lights on this particular dock, and they glow with a golden color.

From time to time the quiet of the early morning is shattered by violent attacks of schools of bigger fish, and I plan to see just what these bigger fish are.

I make a long cast—it is best not to get too close to the lights as the big fish are spooky. My topwater walk-the-dog plug wobbles and gurgles from the darkness into the circle of light cast by one of the dock lights. I let the lure sit and then when I move it, it just disappears—GLURG, and gone.

I let the fish have just a moment with the plug and then I set the hook hard. When I get the slack out I have a big, angry fish on my line, and I am having fun in the darkness.

It takes me a while to work the big fish in—the big ones try hard to make their way back into the dock structure where they can tangle the line and break off. But finally I have a fine, just-above-slot-size redfish rolling alongside my kayak.

I carefully lip the big fish—those treble hooks are dangerous when used by angry redfish as weapons against anglers—and when I lift it into the boat I estimate its weight at eight, maybe nine pounds. At any rate, it is a fine topwater redfish.

As I admire this first fish of the early fall morning there is another violent explosion under the dock lights, and I decide to let this fish go so I can attend to its friends. Some things are so good it's not enough to experience it just once.

Special Considerations

Wolf Creek is pretty easy to get to, and the fishing is generally well worth the traffic that sometimes occurs on Hwy 59. During summertime peak tourist season the traffic around the shopping mall on Hwy 59 can be brutal, especially on rainy days when visitors can't go to the beach.

There are many good places for kayak anglers to find good food during a visit to the Wolf Creek area. Along Hwy 59 the full range of restaurants—both chains and smaller, locally owned eateries—can be found.

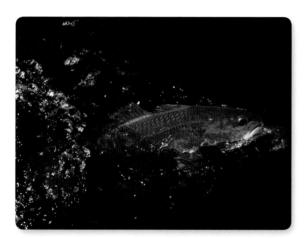

Smaller reds on upper Wolf Creek are reliable targets for kayak anglers.

Wolf Creek—easy to get on the water and good fishing, too.

Local Sources of Information

The best local kayak shop for anglers in need is Fairhope Boat Company (251-928-3417). These folks are very good at repairs and accessories, but the shop is probably thirty miles from Wolf Creek.

Some good local information can be obtained by going to the Mobile Bay Kayak Fishing Association website. The MBKFA folks are always happy to help visitors get good advice about fishing coastal Alabama.

Chris Vecsey at Sam's Bait and Tackle in Orange Beach is an expert kayak angler, and he can help visitors with information about inshore and offshore kayak fishing (251-981-4245). The shop can be found at 27122 Canal Road, Orange Beach, Alabama, 36561.

Great Kayak Fishing Site 8

Perdido Pass, Baldwin County, Alabama

General Site Information

Kayak anglers who take to the clear waters of Perdido Pass can either stay in the pass or move to the backwaters around Ono Island and the shoreline of Orange Beach for reds and specks, or they can paddle or pedal a half-mile through the pass and be in the deep waters of the Gulf and the territory of some really big fish.

Some very good fishing for kayak anglers occurs in the pass itself, around the bridge pilings, and along the massive rock jetties that break the strong surf from the open Gulf and provide protection for the dredged pass.

The Perdido Pass Bridge gives kayak anglers good inshore fishing spots.

Redfish, Spanish mackerel, mangrove snapper, flounder, and even the occasional king mackerel are caught in the pass. In the late fall and winter Perdido Pass has a great sheepshead fishery.

Kayakers can make their way out of the pass—it is not a far run at all. A mile or less takes a kayaker well out into the Gulf and all sorts of big fish possibilities open up. Kayak anglers fishing in the Gulf from Perdido Pass catch kings, big Spanish mackerel, cobias in migration time, and in fall and winter some very big redfish school up just out of the pass.

It is an easy carry from the parking area east of the pass.

How to Access the Area

Exit I-10 at the Loxley exit and drive south on Hwy 59. You will go through Loxley, Robertsdale, and Foley, and you will cross the high bridge over the Intracoastal Canal. Then you'll be in Gulf Shores. When Hwy 59 ends at the stoplight turn left and head east toward Florida.

About ten miles down Beach Road you will cross the high bridge at Perdido Pass—you've made it. The best launch areas are on the east side of the bridge at the park and access areas. It is a short hundred-yard carry to the water at the bridge.

The park offers kayak anglers restrooms and showers, which can be very welcome at most times.

Winter is sheepshead time for Perdido Pass kayak anglers—lots of fun.

A Little Fish Story

The tide was really ripping as it headed toward the Gulf. The waves slopped up against the massive grey granite boulders which make up the jetty breakwater at Perdido Pass. Although it is wintertime by the calendar, here on the Alabama Gulf Coast the expected high for today is over seventy degrees, and it is quite comfortable being on the water. Next week may be windy and downright cold, but today on the coast it's wonderful.

My wife and I were able to find some good live shrimp at a local bait shop—not always easy in winter, so we had good hopes of finding some eager sheepshead who might like to come home with us for a fish supper.

Sheepshead are members of the porgy family of fish and they are absolutely unmistakable. Solid black and white stripes give sheepshead a zebra pattern. And their teeth—well, the teeth of sheepshead are an orthodontist's dream. Big buckteeth and broad crushing molars give this fish an almost human look in a goofy kind of way. Someone way back thought these fish had teeth like a sheep so the name just stuck.

When hooked on light gear a five-pound sheepshead is an absolute blast to catch. They pull hard and they just keep on pulling. Hooking them is an art, and it is not easy. With those massive teeth and a quick "suck in and blow out" action as it feeds, a sheepshead can strip an angler's hook clean in less time than it takes to tell of it. It is truly a challenge to catch sheepies, and that is one reason why I love chasing after them in my kayak.

The other reason I like them? They are delicious fish—just about the best eating fish I have ever found.

So my wife and I were here at the rocks at Perdido Pass and we had supper on our minds. A nice blackened sheepshead supper, that is.

I dropped my hook and sinker with a lively shrimp alongside my kayak and let the boat ease along the rock jetty. This kind of fishing is mostly straight up and down fishing; not much long casting for sheepshead. I felt a slight tap and then it was time to rebait. These black and white convict fish are quick. Another shrimp, another tap, another bare hook.

Finally I managed to keep the slack out of my line enough to feel when the first tap came and I tightened up my line enough so the kahle hook—a specially shaped hook that is very effective on sheepshead—could find a place to bite.

My rod bent, my kayak moved away from the rocks, and I soon had a dandy three-pound sheepshead boat side. I carefully lifted the sheepy into the kayak—they have

This is a fine sheepshead. Kayaks are perfect for fishing the Perdido Pass rock jetties for striped bait stealers.

It is hard to misidentify a sheepshead. These hard fighters are perfect kayak angling targets.

some ferocious spines on their dorsal fins—and then I dropped the unhappy fish in the fish bag behind my kayak seat.

My wife hollered for help. She had a massive sheepshead hooked and it was treating her badly. She did a very good job of hanging on and wearing the fish down. Finally the big old darker-than-usual sheepshead came to the surface and I managed to get a landing net under it. This big old six-pounder was going to provide some excellent fillets.

Supper was looking very positive.

The clear, cool-weather water of Perdido Pass gave up a lot of sheepshead to us that day, but we only kept the first two we caught. Since these fish were running bigger than usual this day two fish provided all the fillets we needed for supper.

And was supper good? Blackened sheepshead is first rate eating always, and after a good day of fishing in Perdido Pass this supper was superb.

Special Considerations

Kayak anglers must be aware that Perdido Pass carries a very heavy load of boat traffic. Hundreds of power boats of all sizes make their way through Perdido Pass on a daily basis, and they can make for some very confused seas with their mixed boat wakes.

Also kayaks can be hard to see when big boat skippers are looking at other big boats, the rock jetties, and the many other things going on in this busy place. Please have warning flags on your kayak and try to stay clear of the channel. Kayaks can go in shallow water—big boats can't.

Kayak anglers can have a blast going to the gulf through Perdido Pass—hold on once you get to the gulf.

Our buddy Tim Perkins, a freshwater bass fishing tournament champion, finds the Alabama Gulf fish a bit of a challenge.

Local Sources of Information

Chris Vecsey works at Sam's Bait and Tackle, 27122 Canal Road in Orange Beach, and he is a very good source of information and advice about the fishing at Perdido Pass and other locations on the Alabama coast (251-981-4245).

Great Kayak Fishing Site 9

Mobile-Tensaw River Delta, Baldwin and Mobile Counties, Alabama

General Site Information

The Mobile Delta is a special place among special places. This is a huge, wild, unsettled tract of land and water that gives kayak anglers opportunity to catch saltwater and freshwater fish at the same time, in the same water, with the same bait.

Kayak anglers can choose to fish the open, saltier water of the upper Mobile Bay, or they can choose to fish fresher water up north, where they can see some classic Deep South bayous, swamps, creeks, and surrounding woodland.

The causeway connecting Mobile and Baldwin counties is the best place for kayak anglers to access the Delta. There are many access points along the causeway, and there are a number of live bait shops that make it quick and easy for kayak anglers to get on the water and after fish.

Meaher Park, a state park located on the causeway, offers campers with kayaks easy and safe access to the Tensaw River from a nice boat ramp. Full camping facilities are provided at Meaher Park, and it is a very good central location for extended exploration of the Delta region. During the Mardi Gras season—usually sometime in February—Meaher Park will totally fill up with parade-goers, but good camping spots are usually open most other times of the year.

In addition to the live bait shops and good access points along the causeway there are several world-class seafood restaurants, and they all welcome kayak anglers for a fine dining experience even if the anglers are straight off the water from fishing.

Depending on the time of year kayak anglers can expect to catch redfish, speckled trout, flounder, ladyfish, and other saltwater species around the causeway, and by paddling a bit farther up the rivers they can expect to encounter largemouth bass, bream of several kinds, some truly massive catfish, and crappie—if it swims in warm water in Alabama it is probably here.

There are five big rivers that feed into the Delta region, and anglers can often find schools of speckled trout chasing shrimp out in the lower parts of the rivers where the fish can be followed and cast to. Catching open water schooling specks is a whole lot of fun. Look for birds diving on bait driven to the surface by the feeding specks below. Anglers can work ditches and feeder creeks—drop-offs at the mouths of these small streams are best—for slot size and smaller redfish.

The delta freshwater bayous are gorgeous places, and kayak anglers do well there.

Big rivers and big fish can be found on the Mobile Delta.

When kayak anglers fish around the causeway and the I-10 bridges—they run parallel and no more than one hundred yards apart in many places as they cross Mobile Bay—they should not be surprised to encounter some big bull redfish and big jack crevalle which make feeding runs up to the wide areas of flats often holding massive schools of pogies and other bait fish.

In short, there are just not many places like the Mobile Delta for kayak anglers who want to try and catch a little of everything. Of course, there are alligators—lots of them—in the Delta.

Yes, there are gators here, too. They don't present much danger to kayak anglers.

Fishing quiet, open water in fall is a great way to collect a mess of speck trout.

How to Access the Area

This is about as easy as it gets. From I-10, take the Spanish Fort exit—a Bass Pro Shop store is at the same exit—and then take the winding access road down the hill where it intersects with the causeway crossing the bay. That's it. Drive until you see a spot that looks good and look for a pull-off and parking area.

A Little Fish Story

I had bought a few dozen shrimp at Scott's Landing, a favorite stop for kayak anglers who visit the Mobile Delta. I launched my kayak from the wooden boardwalk at Scott's and within two minutes I was in fishing water on the Tensaw River.

This warm fall day promised great things: the wind was just enough to help keep biting bugs away and to help keep things a little cooler. Reports had claimed fish were biting here, too.

I paddled down to a favorite fishing spot on the eastern shore of the river. This spot was a big shallow flat with a great many old stumps and old dock pilings left from long gone docks and other landing structures. I could get my kayak through the mine field of underwater obstacles and very few powerboats could, so this was a very good spot for kayak fishing.

I found my favorite old dock piling, tied my kayak up to it, and let the easy current of the river take me just downstream of the piling. A shrimp boat was working out in the main channel of the river between I-10 and the causeway and a cloud of gulls was diving and screaming over the nets as they were pulled and emptied.

I hooked up a nice lively shrimp and cast it into a place of great danger for a shrimp: out into the field of old dock pilings where redfish love to gather and ambush prey as it drifts past.

At this time of year the Delta's waters see a great migration of shrimp and other small delicious things that have spent the summer growing and feeding up in the Delta, and now with coming cooler weather they are making their way out to the open Mobile

In one fishing spot, at one time, on the same bait, we catch redfish . . .

. . . and nice speckled trout . . .

. . . and a big blue catfish. That is kayak fishing on the Mobile Delta.

Bay and Gulf, where they will winter over before returning to the Delta's shallow, fertile water next spring.

This situation gives big game fish a slowly moving banquet of free and easy-to-catch food, and the game fish are eager to belly up to the table and feed.

My bright orange bobber floated gently with the current, and then, almost too quickly to be seen, it just disappeared. Bloop and gone, just like that.

I set the hook and I recognized the strong pull and head shakes of a redfish. I managed to keep the red out of the snags and worked it to the kayak. A nice slot-size red went into the cooler for a fish supper.

Next, I cast the same rig and bait out to the open middle of the river. This time the float jiggled once, then twice, and on the third jiggle it sank out of sight. I started the fish back toward me and the silver-sided speckled trout came to the surface and put on a show of jumping and surface fighting. Fresh speck trout is very, very good, so I dropped this fat two-pounder in the cooler to keep the redfish company.

My next cast went downstream of my kayak over the drop-off where the bottom goes from the shallow flats to the much deeper main channel. This time my float sat there for a while, then it started to move off slowly toward the open water of the river. When the float went under I set the hook and I nearly lost the rod. A very powerful pull came, my rod bent way over, and my level-wind reel gave line steadily to the fish's pull.

Now this fish was big, but it did not fight exactly like a redfish. It was slower, but I just could not turn the fish and slow it down until it had made its way several yards out into the middle of the broad river.

A number of times I moved the big fish back toward me and a number of times the fish just moved back out. I was puzzled, but at last I got the big fish close enough to my kayak that I could see it as it rolled over in the cloudy water.

Loads of fat, delicious bream can be found in the Mobile Delta bayous for kayak anglers to collect.

A very nice—probably ten-pound or so—blue catfish had taken my shrimp. Now, how about this: same place, same bait, three different fish. Both saltwater fish and freshwater fish had come together to eat up the shrimp that were trying to make it to their winter homes.

The big old blue catfish went into the cooler—pretty much filled it right up, too. There was going to be some good eating in my neighborhood this night.

As an afterthought, on my way back to the landing and the parking area I found I had one shrimp left in my bucket—a big old whiskery grandpa shrimp. I pinned it on my hook and lobbed it out as I pedaled under the causeway bridge that crosses the Tensaw River. I was not paying attention and something nearly took my rod out of my hand. I was using my level-wind rig loaded with twenty-five-lb. braid line and a fairly heavy leader, but it made no difference. This fish—and I am sure it was a full grown old blue catfish—just powered its way to the big snag piled up around the support of the bridge and that was that. There is no telling just how big that old catfish was, but for sure he was bigger than I could handle.

Kayak anglers should fish around the cypress trees in spring for some great crappie catching.

You just never know what a kayak angler will catch on the Mobile Delta—this gar gave a very hard fight.

Where do bait shrimp come from? The Mobile Delta supplies much of the bait shrimp for the entire Northern Gulf Coast region.

Special Considerations

For those kayak anglers who are not familiar with the delta, finding out the truth about the insect life there can be shocking. Mosquitoes and no-see-ums can be about as bad on the waters of the delta—especially up past where the salt water goes—as anywhere else in this part of the world. Please go prepared with long sleeves and long pants, and whatever bug repellent that works for you. The bugs will still be there. Fishing at night? Don't even think about it. Some things are not worth even the great fishing found in the Mobile Delta.

The best advice and warning that can be given about kayak fishing in the Mobile Delta is this: never get out of the boat and try to wade! The muddy bottom of the Mobile Delta is sticky and it is deep, and anyone who tries to walk a kayak over a super shallow spot or flat will soon find themselves waist deep in muck and stuck—seriously. Stay in the boat and push or pole, or do whatever you have to do to get over shallow spots, but do not get out and walk.

On the Gulf Coast during winter, tides and water levels tend to run considerably shallower than the rest of the year. On the Mobile Delta, when winter low tides are combined with a strong north wind, vast areas of shallow flats will be found high and at least partly dry. Kayak anglers do not have nearly the problem with this that power boaters do, but we still need to be aware that places where we caught good fish during the summer may now be dry land.

Local Sources of Information

Mobile Bay Kayak Fishing Association (MBKFA.com). This is a very good online source of local fishing information—these are good folks.

Meaher State Park (251-626-5529)

Great Kayak Fishing Site 10

West Fowl River, Mobile County, Alabama

General Site Information

West Fowl River is a short, tidal influenced river that drains part of southern Mobile County, Alabama. It splits from Fowl River—a slightly larger flow—a few miles from the kayak launch spot covered in this book.

West Fowl River has a good deal of boat traffic, both private fishing craft and commercial shrimping and oystering boats. Kayak anglers will need to be aware that these larger and faster boats will be using the same water and that they cannot leave the main channels. No matter where you go kayak fishing on the Gulf Coast, give big commercial fishing boats plenty of space.

West Fowl River empties into the Mississippi Sound, and there are numerous sandbars and oyster bars that larger power craft have to navigate around. Kayaks should have no problem accessing many places where other types of boats cannot.

There is a very good boat launch used by large private fishing boats and working oyster boats; kayak anglers can drop their kayaks, drive a short distance to the parking lot, and be on the water in a matter of moments.

There is attractive mixed coastal forest and low, flat marshes on opposite sides of the river. West Fowl River is small enough and narrow enough to allow kayak anglers

On the west side of Mobile Bay, West Fowl River is a wonderful smaller stream for kayak anglers.

There is a good public launch at the mouth of West Fowl River perfect for kayak anglers.

to find protection from the wind in nearly all conditions, and there are some lovely small bayous which branch off from the main river. These small side streams can hold good redfish at times.

West Fowl River gives kayak anglers the chance to utilize equipment of their choice. Spinning and baitcast gear is standard. Light to medium weight gear will work—twelve-lb. line is just about right. Fly folks can expect to find good fishing here, especially when the wind is down.

Live bait is the standard offering for most species found here. Redfish, speckled trout, flounder, sheepshead, black drum, ladyfish, and mangrove snapper are commonly encountered. When the reds are schooled up tight on rough bottom stuff it helps to fish the shrimp under a popping cork, which keeps the hook up off the bottom and helps limit snags and breakoffs—there are plenty of oyster shells and other sharp structures that can really cost kayak anglers a lot of terminal tackle.

Look for good concentrations of redfish in slightly deeper holes and pockets; these can be hard to find without electronic help from fish finders because the water here is almost always colored to some extent, but if kayak anglers can locate one of these deeper holes chances are redfish will be there.

How to Access the Area

It is a bit involved to reach West Fowl River, but most kayak anglers will think the trip is worth it.

First, exit I-10 west of Mobile via exit 17 and head south on Rangeline Road toward Dauphin Island. Watch your speed on Rangeline Road, it is patrolled heavily. You will cross the bridge over Theodore Industrial Canal—not the best looking water, but kayak anglers have good luck there, especially in the winter.

As you continue on Rangeline it will connect with Hwy 193, and you will drive through commercial development and residential neighborhoods. You'll cross the Fowl River, and all of this time you will be parallel to Mobile Bay, which can be seen through open areas.

Now I know redfish have got to be up in this bayou somewhere.

At the stop light before you start across the big causeway and bridge to Dauphin Island turn right on Hwy 188 and head toward Coden and Bayou Le Batre (yes, there is a real Bayou LeBatre—it was not invented for *Forrest Gump*). After about eight miles you'll turn left on to an unlabeled street—it is a dead end, and it ends at the maintained boat launch area where kayak anglers can put in and paddle down the short canal to the river. By the way, there is a small alligator that lives in the canal, but he will not bother kayak anglers. At least he never has yet.

A Little Fish Story

It was a slow day on the water. My wife and I had launched at the ramp on West Fowl River and we had explored some gorgeous small bayous that looked like they had to be full of hungry redfish. Nothing there.

We had cast live shrimp and a wide selection of lures to the deeper shoreline. Nothing there.

We had paddled up to the old sunken shrimp boat site where lots of bottom cover and deeper water almost always hold fish. Some small croaker bites, but nothing else.

It was a slow day.

West Fowl River gives kayak anglers some very good sheepshead fishing.

Here's the start of an inshore Alabama slam—a nice redfish.

Followed by a good speckled trout.

We started on our defeated way back to the ramp, and as I usually do I had a live shrimp trolling behind me. Kayaks are perfect craft for slow-trolling, whether using lures or live bait. The slow speed of kayaks is perfect for bumping a bait across the bottom of the river, and this puts the bait in perfect locations to find fish. And I did.

I was watching the graceful spirals and turns of a big flock of pelicans as they circled high above us, riding the light southern breeze with perfect skill and grace. As I admired the flight of pelicans my rod was nearly pulled from my hand. I tightened my grip, my rod bent over double, and I could feel the strong tail pumps and head shakes of a good fish. Of course I was using the lightest rig I had—that's the way it always works with big fish—and my reel's drag made funny squealing noises as it gave line to the powerful runs of the fish.

My kayak was slowly pulled out to the middle of the river by the fish and I was able to start the fish back to the kayak before it made another strong run.

Finally I got the fish to the kayak, and sure enough, there flashed the broad bronze sides and the black spot on the wide tail—a redfish, and a good one.

This upper slot size red would weigh seven or eight pounds—a lovely fish, and since we were not hungry for fish this West Fowl River redfish got another life.

I re-baited, cast back out, and started my slow pedal back toward the dock. Twice in quick succession I had good strikes and fine one-to-two-pound speckled trout fell to my slow open water troll.

I got a nibbling bite and I managed to set the hook in the tough, toothy mouth of a sheepshead. Its black and white stripes and human-looking teeth flashed in the afternoon light.

As we neared the canal to pull out and head home I felt one last strike, and moments later I had a slightly undersize flounder in the boat. I had managed to catch a red, a speck, and a flounder all on the same day—that's called an "Inshore Slam" down here on the coast, and it does not happen every day.

Slow trolling was the ticket, and it often is. Places like West Fowl River are perfect for this kind of fishing. The water is not super deep, it is generally protected from the wind, and kayak anglers can slowly pedal or paddle along the channels and go just fast enough to have the lure or bait make regular contact with the bottom.

The fish will do the rest.

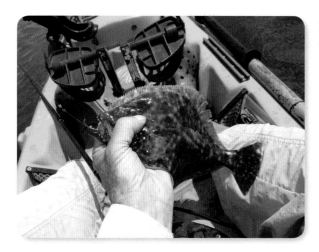

And then a small flounder. This is the way we do it on West Fowl River.

Special Considerations

West Fowl River is very representative of the many, many tributary streams that empty into Mobile Bay and related waters. This means that at certain times biting bugs can be fierce. A particularly nasty brand of no-see-ums calls the West Fowl River area home, and they can make life miserable for kayak anglers. Make sure you have good insect repellent, and long sleeves and pants may be needed.

Rough water conditions are not much of a problem here since the river is generally protected by trees and large areas of open marsh. However, a very strong southwest wind can make West Fowl River pretty rough for kayak anglers.

Kayak anglers will need to be aware of other larger and faster boats—a good elevated warning flag is always a good idea.

For those who are not familiar with the Alabama Gulf Coast, it might be tempting to pull up one of the many crab traps which have round marker floats just to see what is inside. Please *do not do this*! If the owner of the trap happens to be in the area and sees a stranger messing with his traps there will be trouble. Crabbers are hard-working people, and they resent anyone disturbing their traps. If you should happen to accidentally hook a crab trap while fishing just break your line and move away.

Local Sources of Information

My buddy Captain Yano Serra (251-610-0462 or Speck-Tackle-Lure.com) is starting to run kayak mother ship trips on the waters of western Mobile Bay. He is licensed in Alabama and Mississippi, and he knows these waters as well as such a vast and varied area can be known. He is a great man to call and see about a guided kayak trip to the Mobile Bay system and the Mississippi Sound.

Kayak anglers can find some very good advice on the Mobile Bay Kayak Fishing Association forum. The folks who operate and contribute to the MBKFA are happy to help visitors find good fishing.

Notes

Mississippi offers kayak anglers some wonderful backwater bayous for paddling and fishing.

I like Mississippi. There is good fishing, and there is some very good food there, too. The folks are friendly, and it is not hard to get a kayak on the water anywhere along the coast in Mississippi. Most inshore fishing in Mississippi gives kayakers a very good chance to fish water that not many other anglers have fished hard recently.

As the kayak angler travels across Mississippi on I-10 several rivers will be crossed: the Wolf, the Pearl, the Pascagoula, the Escatawpa, and my favorite name for a river, the Tchoutacabouffa. They all have good freshwater and mixed water fishing for kayak anglers.

However, the barrier islands lying offshore of the Mississippi mainland are

Redfish are thick in Mississippi coastal waters, and they fight hard like all reds.

the primary focus of most kayak anglers; these are some wonderful places for kayak folks to paddle to and catch some big, mean fish.

There are plenty of chain stores along the Mississippi coast for general supplies and camping needs, and there is at least one first-rate kayak shop near I-10—Everything Kayaks—which can help visiting folks out in time of need.

Traffic is not usually too bad in Mississippi. On I-10 it can get rough on holiday weekends and normal rush hours during the week, but generally it is easy to get around.

Highway 90 runs parallel to the gulf, and this is the road most kayak anglers will want to use to find launch spots along the coast. There are plenty of pull-offs and parking spots along the beaches in Biloxi, Gulfport, and Long Beach.

From Pascagoula on the east to Pass Christian and other points to the west, the coast of Mississippi offers kayak anglers good access and good fishing.

Throw a shrimp near a Mississippi speck and see what happens.

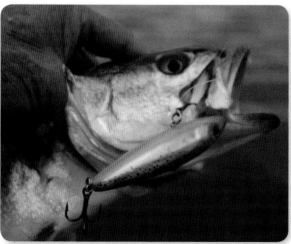

Look for diving birds and Mississippi trout will probably be feeding under them.

Housing for Visitors

One thing that sets Mississippi apart from the other states and waters covered in this book is the wide range of housing for visiting kayak anglers to occupy. Everything from low budget chain motels to really high-class condos and beach homes can be found along the Mississippi coast.

But the biggest difference between the Mississippi coast and the other spots we are looking at is the casinos. There are a number of massive casinos and resorts which line the waterfront from Biloxi to Long Beach, and for kayak anglers who are gamblers at heart, these casinos might be very good things to consider. It seems possible to launch a kayak early in the morning, catch some reds and specks, and then paddle back, take a shower, and go to the tables for some fun. Staying at a casino for a kayak fishing trip might be a good possibility for those kayak anglers who have non-fishing family members along on the trip; there's a lot of non-fishing stuff to do at the casinos, too.

Food—Reason Enough to Come Here

One of the reasons I like Mississippi so much is there are many food choices here, and they are all good.

There are many seafood restaurants along the coast, and there's a strong Cajun influence here, so the seafood is just natural-born good.

Mississippi has recovered from the devastation of Hurricane Katrina, and it is a great destination for kayak anglers.

And the food in Mississippi? Just about the best seafood Po-boys to be found anywhere.

If you can't find some good food in Mississippi you're not trying very hard.

In Ocean Springs, BB's Po'Boys and Seafood (1300 Bienville Blvd, 228-875-2702)—a small, privately owned and operated seafood restaurant—makes the best po-boy sandwiches I have ever found, and that is saying a great deal. By the way, if you don't know what a po'boy is you have a life thrill coming.

It is worth the time to take a short drive through old Biloxi. It lies just off Hwy 90 as you cross the high Biloxi Bay Bridge. There are strong Vietnamese and other oriental influences there, and some superb French bakeries and other restaurants can also be found.

In short, the eating is very good in southern Mississippi.

Notes

Great Kayak Fishing Site 11

Petit Bois Island, offshore Jackson County, Mississippi

General Site Information

Kayak fishing this easternmost and second largest of Mississippi's chain of gorgeous offshore barrier islands is an adventure. This is not a trip for a spur of the moment, casual fishing jaunt. Even though Petit Bois is only nine miles or so off the coast it is isolated, and there are no services of any kind on the island.

Petit Bois gives kayak anglers the chance to catch some great redfish and trout, and when conditions are favorable, kayak anglers can fish the open Gulf side for king mackerel, big crevalle jacks, bull redfish, and tarpon in season. Some very big sharks inhabit the waters around Petit Bois, so kayak anglers need to make sure their fishing gear is up to the task.

The north side of the island is usually more protected from the dominant south winds, and there are some fine shallow flats with good grass beds for early morning and late evening topwater fishing for reds and specks.

Fishing the cuts and gulleys that run out from the south side of the island toward the open Gulf can provide some very fast, very intense fishing for big schools of redfish that sweep through the area looking for food.

Petite Bois is a good place for kayak anglers to find tripletail—a very unusual looking fish that provides a great fight. These big, dark-colored fish will be found holding very close to any sort of floating object: crab trap buoys, floating logs, or even just any kind of floating trash. They will look like shadows under the floating stuff, and they will welcome a live shrimp or an artificial worked right in their faces.

Tripletail are hard fighting fish that will challenge kayak anglers around Petit Bois Island.

Petit Bois Island gives anglers unsettled, undeveloped fishing, and lots of big fish.

How to Access the Area

There are basically two ways to get to Petit Bois. First, if the kayak angler is up for a nine-mile open water paddle it is easy to launch at Pascagoula, Mississippi, and paddle south to reach the island. Please keep in mind there are no services of any kind on Petit Bois, so the kayaker must take water, food, protection, and gear along. To be honest, I am not up to this level of effort.

The second way to access the island is to contact a guide—I highly recommend Captain Yano Serra of Coden, Alabama—who can transport the kayak and kayaker to the island and then pick everything up and bring everyone back home at the end of the trip. This allows the kayak angler to reach the island in good shape and not exhausted from the long paddle out.

Pascagoula can be reached by exiting I-10 at exit 69 and taking Hwy 63 south to reach the park and launch area. Captain Yano generally departs from Bayou Le Batre in Alabama.

A Little Fish Story

I had long wanted to fish Petit Bois Island, but I knew I could not make the extended paddle required to reach the offshore barrier island—my long distance paddling days are over. So when my buddy, Captain Yano Serra of Coden, Alabama, invited me to get a lift out to Petit Bois in his guide boat I jumped at the chance.

We departed from Bayou Le Batre, Alabama, and as we cruised at speed out past the isolated low sand islands and entered Mississippi state waters, I realized just how hard it would be for me to paddle out to Petit Bois. But in his boat it was a very short run—just twelve miles—and then we arrived.

Petit Bois lay totally wild and free from any sort of human development. A forest of tough pine trees and low scrub brush covered the higher inshore parts of the island and the beaches glowed with the brilliant white sand this part of the world is so famous for.

On the north side of Petit Bois, kayak anglers should work the gullies and ditches for some fine redfish.

The wind was light and from the north on this early spring day, so we chose to fish the southern side of Petit Bois. There was a low, remnant swell from the Gulf, but it was not a problem for our boat or kayak. When conditions are right fishing Petit Bois can be an absolute pleasure.

I cast my ¼-oz. jig and scented soft grub tail in the darker water of one of the many cuts which drain water back to the Gulf after waves break on the beach. Then I saw what looked like a shadow sweeping across the shallower, lighter colored sand toward the deeper water I was fishing.

I let my jig sink to the bottom, and when the shadow reached the deeper water I gave the jig a hop, and then things got interesting.

I felt a sharp strike, and then my reel began to make that noise that means only one thing: a big redfish has come to visit. I held on—there is not much else to do at this point—and the hooked red pulled drag and stripped line off my reel.

One of the very best things about hooking a large fish from a kayak is that the kayak and its light weight allow the fish to pull the boat, thus the angler's gear never

This may be the best way for kayak anglers to reach Petit Bois Island. Make sure all gear is off-loaded and that the tow rope is secure.

Captain Yano Serra will transport kayak anglers to Petit Bois, and he can advise kayak anglers on where and how to fish once there.

Lots of reds call Petit Bois home, and kayak anglers can load up on the hard pullers there.

reaches the breaking point. The fish pulled and pulled, and my kayak moved slowly with the fish, helping to tire it out.

Finally I got my red—it was a semi-bull, about twelve pounds or so—to the side of the kayak, where it finned in the clear water. I took a few photos, removed the hook, and sent the big red on its way.

Captain Yano had stayed aboard his guide boat—he is not totally convinced about this kayak fishing thing yet—and I saw he had hooked something big on his fly rod.

I moved closer to the battle and I watched Yano expertly work his big redfish with the long rod. After a while he managed to get the big red to the boat and he lifted it aboard. It is a truly fine place when anglers can hook and catch bull redfish on fly rods, in my opinion, and Petit Bois is that kind of place.

I went back to the deeper water gulley where I had hooked my first redfish, and when I got within casting distance I tossed my jig and grub back into the darker water where the current was moving back out to the Gulf.

This time my jig never made it to the bottom before something big and bad intercepted it. Second verse same as the first; this Petit Bois redfish angling is some fun stuff.

I fought this fish for a while. Yano hooked and caught another big red. We had a great morning.

As we motored back to the docks at Bayou le Batre I asked Yano if he had ever considered a camping trip to Petit Bois for some kayak fishing. He laughed and said, "I'm thinking about it right now."

Special Considerations

Petit Bois Island is a gorgeous place and the kayak fishing can be superb, but anglers need to keep in mind that even though it is only nine miles or so offshore there are no services of any kind on the island; it is uninhabited and undeveloped, so everything needed must be transported. Any kayak angler considering a paddle out and paddle back trip should make sure that adequate emergency supplies—and this absolutely includes lots of drinking water—are aboard.

Also, if weather should deteriorate anglers may be stuck on the island for longer than planned.

Here is some good advice: *Do not attempt a trip to Petit Bois in bad weather.* The weather needs to be settled with very low storm potential. The Mississippi Sound is wide open and a wind can develop a nasty swell and chop very quickly here.

NOAA operates a weather monitoring station on the west end of Petit Bois Island. This station generates current condition updates which can be reached online (http://www.ndbc.noaa.gov/station page php?station=ptbm6). The National Marine Service also provides good weather updates (gcrl.usm.edu/public'weather.php).

Petit Bois does have alligators in the lagoons and ponds of the interior of the island, and there are snakes—some are nasty. The biggest wildlife problem kayak anglers are likely to encounter are the bugs. Mosquitoes, blackflies, deer flies, and no-see-ums all call the island home, and they can be fierce.

In short, a kayak fishing trip to Petit Bois can be a wonderful experience. An extended camping trip to Petit Bois could be a very memorable trip. However, it has the potential to be pretty awful, too. Make good plans and preparations and have backup plans.

Local Sources of Information

Visiting kayak anglers to the Mississippi coast can get good information from Mississippi Kayak Fishing Forum (mskayakfishing.com). These are good folks who can provide up-to-the-minute advice and directions on what is biting and where, and also kayak fishing get togethers.

There is a very good kayak shop in Gulfport, Mississippi, Everything Kayak, at 15240 Creosote Road (228-865-1000 or www.everythingkayak.com).

To contact Captain Yano Serra:
251-610-0462
Speck-tackle-lure.com

Great Kayak Fishing Site 12

Deer Island, Hancock County, Mississippi

General Site Information

Anglers who paddle or pedal a very short distance off the beach at Biloxi can be fishing some very good water in a remarkably short time.

Deer Island—actually not one of Mississippi's barrier islands—is separated from the mainland by a quickly crossed, narrow channel used by craft of all sizes. This means that kayak anglers can find some good fishing without the long and involved paddle or transit to the real barrier islands. And despite being very close to the mainland and its casinos, traffic, and noise, kayak anglers can find and catch some very good—and in some cases very big—fish.

Kayak anglers should pay attention to the rock jetties on the west end of Deer Island. These rock structures can hold some very good fish, including redfish and speckled trout. In fact, when kayak fishing the Gulf Coast, any water that has rock structure has the potential to be a fishing hotspot.

In the open water of the channel separating Deer Island from the mainland, kayak anglers can find schools of small specks chasing shrimp and minnows to the surface where they attract the attention of terns and other birds. Keep an eye for these diving, screaming birds, because there's a reason they are acting that way: food is under them.

It is a very easy carry from the parking area to the water for Deer Island kayak anglers.

That's Deer Island in the background. It is so close to the main road, but it is so nice once kayakers arrive there.

Another good idea for kayak anglers who fish Deer Island is to paddle their 'yak across the channel, drag the boat across the narrow island—it is quite narrow in many places—and access the open water of the Gulf. This puts kayak anglers in the big game regions where some large redfish, jack crevalle, sharks, and other serious hard pullers live. (This should only be done in fairly flat water conditions and not attempted if there is much surf running.)

Deer Island screens the narrow channel from the worst of the Gulf surf, and this is a good place to go kayak fishing even when the Gulf is too rough for most kayak anglers to try and get on for fishing.

The waters on all sides of Deer Island can be very good for flounder, and there is nothing better for catching flounder than a live bull minnow (these can be found at most local bait and tackle shops or caught in seine nets along the shore). Finger mullet also work very well. Drag these live baits along the bottom behind a ½-oz. sinker, and when the flounder strike comes let the flatfish chew on the bait for a few seconds before setting the hook.

How to Access the Area
From I-10 take exit 50 and head south on Hwy. 57. When Hwy 57 reaches Hwy 90 at Ocean Springs turn right and head west. Soon the very high bridge that crosses Biloxi

Here is a perfect supper. Flounder look funny, but they are just about the best eating fish on the Gulf Coast.

For visiting kayak anglers new to the coast, do not get your fingers near a flounder's mouth! Lots of very sharp teeth there.

Bay will be seen. Deer Island is the pine-covered strip of land that lies just offshore. Drive past the first set of casinos and in about a mile a very good launch area with ramps and parking will be found. This launch area is directly across from the silver metal odd looking building which houses a very nice museum of art. There is good parking at this launch area.

A Little Fish Story

My, goodness, it's already getting hot, but what else should I expect on a day in the middle of July on the Gulf Coast? When I park the car and walk across the parking lot to the sandy beach where I unloaded our kayaks and gear, I work up a sweat.

But there is flat, smooth water pockmarked by schools of pogies and other bait fish, and this is a good sign for fishing. Where there's bait, there are usually big fish to eat it.

Along the Biloxi and Gulfport beaches kayak anglers can find lots of casinos—good places to stay and eat, and maybe win some big bucks.

It is so easy paddling from the beach out toward the low trees and scrub brush of Deer Island, and I slow troll a jig and soft plastic grub behind me as we go. About halfway across the narrow channel separating the mainland and its noise and bustle from the quiet and calm of Deer Island my rod takes a sharp bend and the reel gives a little line, but whatever struck didn't stick. Too bad—that felt like a good fish.

I slow troll along the white sand beach of Deer Island, and after a bit I notice that my wife and daughter have beached their kayaks and started the short walk across the island to look at the Gulf side. Since I am not wearing myself down with catching action I decide to join them.

Even though Deer Island is so close to the busy traffic of Hwy 90 and the folks going to work and the casinos for games of chance and eating the casinos' buffets, here on the island it is a totally different world. Once we are screened by the pine trees and lower brush it seems we are a long, long way from the regular world and its demands.

This is nice. I decide I could stay here for a while under the shade of a big pine tree and just watch the ospreys and pelicans as they go about their business diving and catching fish. But there's something that demands my attention.

About fifty yards off the beach there is a big slick on the surface of the calm water. This slick is caused by something—or a lot of somethings—eating smaller bait fish. As the smaller fish are devoured they release oil; this oil floats to the top and creates a slick which can be seen for quite a distance. Fishing slicks for specks, reds, Spanish mackerel, and other voracious game fish is a very reliable technique all along the Gulf Coast when the water is flat and not rough, and I am not about to let this particular slick go by without trying it out, so I run back and start the short drag with my kayak across the white sand.

When I arrive back on the south side I quickly ease the kayak into the water, push it off until it floats, and then I step in. With a few paddle strokes I am within casting range of the slick and whatever is feeding below.

I make a cast and I let the jig and soft plastic trailer sink to the bottom—it is only four feet deep or so here. I start the slow hop-hop-hop retrieve to make the jig look like something moving along the bottom. Sure enough I get a sharp tap, and then another sharp tap, and then the jig just seems to stop. If this is what I hope it is eating the jig I do not want to be in a hurry at this point. I let the jig sit still, and when I gently move the jig in a few moments I feel a solid pressure. Then I set the hook with a sharp sideways jerk of the rod. That is when things start to happen.

Whatever I have hooked does not want to come in, and I have a fight with something strong that hugs the bottom and pulls with short, powerful runs. I work the hooked fish

The south side of Deer Island—away from the mainland—is very nice and quiet for kayak anglers to find some good fish.

closer, and just as I hoped, I see the broad, round, dark brown topside of a very good flounder. These strange looking fish are vicious predators, and despite their weird appearance are just about the best eating in the Gulf. I play the good two-pound flounder to the boat, and here is where I have to be careful. Many flounder are lost right at boat side as they put on a final flurry of fighting and rolling. This one stays on the hook and I am happy to lift it into the kayak, where it can be safely deposited in a fish bag.

I move my kayak back in casting range of the spreading slick and fire off another long range cast. I let the jig sink, but this time, just as it reaches the bottom, I feel a sharp strike and a good run starts immediately. Although I am not sure what this fish is, I have hopes it is another flounder. There's not much better eating than fresh flounder grilled up, and I would love to have a flounder supper tonight.

Sure enough, an even better flounder rolls up at boat side and I carefully reach for the line, then carefully lift the fat fish over the kayak . . . and the hook falls out and the flounder falls . . . right in my lap. I grab the struggling flounder and carefully hold it by the gills until it quits squirming. Trying to grab a flounder by the lower jaw is a mistake most anglers will make only once. Flounder have some awfully big, sharp teeth in their mouths and they will bring some blood from anglers who are careless.

Now this is fine. My wife and daughter are starting to make movement back toward their kayaks on the north side of the island, and since I've got enough fish for supper I decide to go with them.

As I reach the north side where they are putting back in to paddle to the launch area, I discover something else about fishing so close to the big casinos and their restaurants: when they start cooking for the big lunch rush of folks staying at the casinos the delicious scent of Gulf Coast seafood and other good eating comes quite clear to anyone on the water close at hand. My belly begins to tell me that it would like something good, too.

So we race across the channel, I back the truck down, and we quickly load the kayaks, tie them in securely, stow the fishing gear, put my fine Deer Island flounder in an ice chest, and go looking for some Po-Boy sandwiches down the road at Ocean Springs.

I could get to like this kind of close in, low pressure Mississippi Gulf Coast fishing.

Special Considerations

Deer Island is one of the safest and easiest fishing locations for a kayak angler to attempt. This is a very good location for less experienced kayak anglers to try. However, the channel separating the island from the mainland is narrow, and lots of big powerboats use the channel on a daily basis as they leave their dockage and head for offshore waters. Kayak anglers need to keep an eye open for big boats.

Of course, a personal flotation device (PFD) must be worn at all times when fishing Gulf Coast waters.

Local Sources of Information

Mississippi Kayak Fishing website (www.mskayakfishing.com). This is a good local website and forum that gives visiting kayak anglers good advice and directions for fishing Mississippi.

Great Kayak Fishing Site 13

Cat Island, offshore Gulfport, Mississippi

General Site Information

Cat Island is the westernmost of the barrier islands off the mainland of Mississippi. This island is largely privately owned, but it is maintained in a pristine, non-developed manner, and it offers visiting kayak anglers a glimpse of the way the barrier islands looked before many of them were modified by human presence.

By the way, Cat Island got its name from the earliest European explorers—the French—who noticed the large number of raccoons on the island, and since they thought the critters were cats that is the name they gave the island. And the raccoons are still there.

Cat Island gives kayak anglers great chances to catch specks, reds, flounder, and big open gulf fish when fishing on the south side of the island. On the southern gulf side kayak anglers catch tripletail, cobia, and sharks on the near shore structure.

There are several big bayous offering some fine sight fishing for reds pushing water and tailing over oyster shell reefs. Kayak anglers should not rush through a promising looking shoreline—fish the shore carefully, because some very big reds come in to the shallow water of the Cat Island bayous, and they often lie still and silent,

Sunrise over Cat Island—a wonderful start to a day spent kayak fishing.

Cat Island's bayous are perfect for kayak anglers.

waiting for a crab or shrimp or finger mullet to come close. Kayak anglers can connect with these big reds, but the big ones will not tolerate much rapid movement or disruption around them.

The usual live shrimp under a popping cork works very well at Cat Island, but we have had very good results fishing slow sink hard plastic jerk baits like the Mirrolure Mirodine lures. Work these hard lures in open water and work them all the way to the boat. Some big specks and reds have followed these lures all the way back to the kayak and then struck just as the lure was being lifted from the water for the next cast.

When the surf allows on the south side of the island kayakers can either pull their 'yaks across a narrow part of the island and fish the surf or just leave the kayak and walk to the surf side and wade fish. Be advised, there are some big sharks around Cat Island, so do not keep your caught fish on a short stringer.

How to Access the Area

It is possible for a strong paddler to launch from the Gulfport and Long Beach beaches and paddle to Cat Island: it is a little over six miles from beach to island. I am past this level of paddling, but a local kayak fishing group—The Pirates of Cat Island— take paddling and camping trips to Cat Island several times each year. The best way to access Cat Island is to contact a local guide who runs mothership trips and have a powerboat load you and the 'yak up, take you to the island, and then bring you back home when you are done for the day.

Transport services will take kayak anglers and their gear quickly to Cat Island from the mainland. *S. Schindler*

Cat Island is a great destination for groups of kayak anglers. *S. Schindler*

Captain Sonny Shindler and his guides with Shorething Charters guide these mothership trips to Cat Island, and he also offers anglers really cool two-, three-, and four-day overnight trips. Captain Sonny has a house—it's more like a mansion—on Cat Island that he takes anglers to for overnight all inclusive trips. This is a wonderful way to experience wild barrier island fishing and then go home to super comfortable surroundings for the night.

To reach the beaches at Gulfport, anglers need to take the Hwy 49 exit off I-10 and follow Hwy 49 through the old town of Gulfport. Take a right at the light on Hwy 90—the beach road—and Long Beach will be alongside the road in just a few miles.

Cat Island is usually quite visible out in the gulf—look for the line of pine trees on the southern horizon.

A Little Fish Story

This morning is overcast but warm, and the water of Cat Island's North Bayou is smooth as I work my way down the shoreline casting a slow sinking jerk bait. This water looks too good this morning for me to not catch any fish, but that is what has happened so far: no hits, no runs, no errors—and no fish.

Off to the north I can see the dark line of the mainland, and a commercial barge and push boat is making its way westward toward Lake Pontchartrain and New Orleans. The world is a good place this morning.

It is quiet except for the birds.

And then, when I have a long cast nearly retrieved and back to the boat, the water swirls and boils behind my bait as a very big redfish makes a pass at my lure. There is no contact—the red missed the lure—but this incident is very promising.

I approach a little point of land I suspect has an oyster reef which continues the shallow point of land out into the bayou, and when I cast over this oyster bar my lure does not sink far before I feel a firm strike and then the dance of desperation of a hooked two-pound speckled trout.

Now this is more like it. For the next thirty minutes I spend time casting, hooking, and catching several fine specks all from this one oyster bar and shoreline area. The specks must be stacked up thick right here. When a kayak angler finds a spot like this, where the fish are ganged up and aggressive, some of the best fishing most anglers will ever experience can happen, and often does.

Of course something always happens at times like this to shut down the bite, and the thing that happens today is a slight breeze has pushed me too close to the shallow

Redfish? You can bet they are at Cat Island, and there are some very big ones there, too. *S. Schindler*

Topwater trout are aggressive in the Cat Island bayous.

Here, house-visiting kayak anglers stay in on one of Captain Sonny Schindler's overnight trips—not too bad at all we'd say. *S. Schindler*

oyster reef; when my kayak floats over the area the bite just quits.

I should have put down the stakeout pole, but I was too busy enjoying myself and this hot, hot trout bite. I resolve to let the trout have a rest here and then I will come back later when they are eating again.

But as I work my way down the bayou toward the broad mouth of the bay where it enters the open Mississippi Sound I manage to find just enough specks and the occasional redfish to make me forget about going back to the hot oyster bar and the specks I found there.

I make one last cast out toward more open water and the water behind my lure swirls and boils as something big and mean and coppery-red takes my lure for a ride—and he pulls me in my kayak for a little ride, too.

This redfish is not a huge fish—maybe ten pounds—but he is strong and determined not to be taken in easily. It is best at times like this

Big flounder are caught by Cat Island kayak anglers. *S. Schindler*

to just hold on, let the rod, reel, and light kayak do their work, and enjoy the free ride.

When the redfish is finally tired out and rolling white belly up beside my kayak I look again to the north and there is the mainland—where folks are going to work, worrying about paying bills, and trying to get ahead.

And I am out here at Cat Island catching trout and redfish. Sometimes things work out the way they are supposed to work out.

Special Considerations

Paddling to Cat Island is doable, but it is only doable if the weather is good, the winds are light, and there is no chance of bad weather developing. Getting halfway to Cat Island in a kayak with a bad storm coming up could be a very desperate time.

Also, there are no services or supplies of any kind at Cat Island for visitors: no water, no food, no supplies. If a self-contained trip is being considered everything needed on the trip will have to go on the kayak. This kind of trip could be memorably good for those paddlers equipped and able to make the long paddle, but it needs to be planned carefully and with a very sharp eye out for bad weather development.

The biting bugs at Cat Island can be ferocious, so regardless of what kind of trip and transportation to the island is planned bug repellant is a primary need.

Local Sources of Information

Captain Sonny Schindler
www.shorethingcharters.com
228-342-2206

Everything Kayak
15240 Creosote road
Gulfport, Mississippi 39503
228-865-1000
www.everythingkayak.com

Notes

LOUISIANA

"Don't you spill dose shrimp! Dey too good to waste!"
Eating seafood is serious business in Louisiana.

L et me go ahead and say what I feel to be the truth: Louisiana has the best coastal and inshore fishing to be found anywhere. There, now we can get on with specifics. Kayak anglers can find the best redfishing in the world from Biloxi Marsh on the east to Lakes Charle on the west. In fact, lower Louisiana seems designed and built with kayak anglers in mind.

What Kinds of Kayak Fishing

In Louisiana kayak anglers can find big, open water places like Lake Ponchartrain, Venice, Caminada Pass at Grand Isle, and Lake Calcasieu, but most kayak anglers will focus on the smaller, more intimate bayous and creeks all along the coast of Louisiana. There are more small paddle waters here than any kayak angler could get to and fish in several lifetimes.

Louisiana seafood is just about the best, and Cajun cooks know what to do with it.

Louisiana is the best place in the world for sight fishing for reds—bar none.

Now, kayak anglers not familiar with the Louisiana coastal area may not be prepared for water conditions here. This is not clear, sandy-bottom water. Louisiana water is cloudy, and the bottom is universally mud—not so good for wading.

However, the cloudy water of Louisiana is alive with things of all sizes and variety that provide food for redfish, speckled trout, flounder, and a host of other game fish. The cloudy water of the Louisiana coastline is a soup of living things, and some of these living things get really big and bad, and will provide a kayak angler with a lot of fun.

Louisiana is the place for a kayak angler who is also a fly rod angler. Louisiana reds are not spooky—I have heard them called "dumb"—and most of the time fly rodders on a kayak can get quite close enough to feeding reds to make a good cast and then receive a violent strike from one. I love fly fishing in Louisiana.

Housing for Visitors

Louisiana has a vibrant tourism industry, so the entire state is set up to accommodate visitors. Along the I-10 and other major corridors kayak anglers will find the full range of chain motels.

As anglers get off the main roads and highways lots of privately owned and operated places to stay will show up.

When the kayak angler gets nearer the coast other possibilities like up-scale fishing lodges can be found.

There should be no problem finding good places to stay in Louisiana.

Other Things to Do

Louisiana is a birder's paradise, especially during the fall migrations. Birds of all kinds will enter the Louisiana coastal regions, and birders can see some birds that may not be easily found at any other time and place. There are also several water bird rookeries that are protected and made open to the public for birders to see during nesting season.

The Cajun tourism business is huge in Louisiana, and those who like zydeco and traditional Cajun music will have a ball in spots like Breaux Bridge and other small towns along the Atchafalaya Region.

Birders who visit Louisiana will have a ball. Ospreys are impressive birds and are common here.

Pink birds? You bet, Louisiana has lots of roseate spoonbills which nest here.

On the Big Muddy, visiting kayak anglers can see New Orleans paddle wheelers touring the city's sights.

Of course there is always food. I love to visit Louisiana and look for little mom and pop places to eat. There's seafood, there's barbecue, and there's home-style country food done Cajun style—there is a lot of good, good food in Louisiana.

We would like to recommend the small town Abbeville as a good place to visit and dine. There are several seafood and Cajun restaurants there and they are all very, very good. And then there is New Orleans.

There is no place in the United States quite like New Orleans. If there's any location more designed for folks to have fun I am not aware of it. But besides the bars and other less exalted activities the aquarium at New Orleans is world-class, and if kids are along on a kayak fishing trip they will love it.

I like to visit New Orleans and try new places to eat. Eating is an art form in New Orleans, and it is fun to see what kinds of food can be found.

It is a lot of fun to sit on the benches in the parks in the French Quarter and just watch people go by. You can see all kinds of people in New Orleans, and the street entertainers are a real experience in and of themselves. It's a constantly changing show in New Orleans.

And even though the French Quarter of New Orleans has been much cleaned up and civilized from its wild and more-than-slightly-decadent past since the horrible arrival of Hurricane Katrina, it would be a very good idea to make sure that all your kayaks and other equipment are very securely locked up before leaving the car and going to see the sights of the Big Easy.

Louisiana—more places to go kayak fishing than we will ever be able to visit, but we can try to see them all.

Notes

Great Kayak Fishing Site 14

Biloxi Marsh, St. Bernard Parish, Louisiana

General Site Information

The Biloxi Marsh is a massive place (more than 210,000 acres) that sits on the border between Mississippi and Louisiana, and it has some of the best redfish and best redfishing in the world. It is not overwhelmed with anglers for a number of reasons. That's the good news.

It is also not easy to actually get to Biloxi Marsh—that is the bad news. In fact, for kayak anglers it is pretty darned difficult to get to the Biloxi Marsh unless we take a mothership trip and overnight stay at the marsh. Of course, a mothership trip is one of the finest ways known to go kayak fishing—it is a wonderful way to enjoy some superb fishing water and spend off-the-water time in very comfortable surroundings.

The Biloxi Marsh lies quite a distance away from any place kayak anglers can access easily, and it is a whole lot farther off than I want to pedal or paddle, but if a kayak angler can book a trip on an overnight stay-aboard big boat it can be one of the most fantastic trips imaginable.

If a kayak angler can get to the marsh and get their kayak in the water, the redfishing in Biloxi Marsh can be hard to believe. The side bayous and ponds off the main channels that criss-cross the massive marsh offer some world-class sight fishing for tailing reds

It is a good thing cold doesn't show up on photographs—these great bayous would be blue in that cold, cold wind.

Here is the mothership—a floating mansion for visiting kayak anglers.

and reds pushing wakes as they chase shrimp and minnows and other small stuff through the shallow water.

For fly rod anglers, Biloxi Marsh can be simply mind-blowing with the sheer number of reds and the lack of concern they seem to have about kayaks and anglers in their vicinity.

Reds are not the only target in Biloxi Marsh. In the larger, more open waters some fine speckled trout can be found, and they will often be under flocks of working birds that clue in on the underwater feeding activity that drives shrimp and minnows to the surface where the birds can take their share.

By fishing soft plastic jigs across the bottom anglers can find and catch some delicious flounder.

One of the best things about fishing the Biloxi Marsh on a mothership trip is how nice the accommodations are and how good the food is for anglers. It truly is a lifetime trip to spend three days on a floating palace of a mothership in the marsh chasing big, mean fish. If it sounds like I am pushing these overnight trips—well, I am. These are truly grand fishing trips.

It's cold, but we are eating Cajun seafood, so we'll be warm inside and very happy.

How to Access the Area

This can be interesting. If visiting kayak anglers book a mothership trip, they will have to meet the transfer boat—usually a big, smooth-running pontoon boat—which will take them and their 'yaks from the dock area to the mothership. Some of these chartered trips leave from Biloxi, Mississippi, and some leave from Shell Beach, Louisiana. The charter folks will give you specific directions, but almost all points of departure will involve exiting from I-10 at some point.

Now, for kayak anglers who cannot afford a mothership trip—and they are not cheap, be warned—it is possible to get the smallest idea of what the

The wind was cold but the food was great, and the beds were warm and soft—this may be a great kayak fishing trip after all.

fantastic fishing in the Marsh is like by putting your kayak in at Shell Beach, Louisiana, and paddling out toward the massive old wreck of Fort Beauregard, a Civil War-era fort built to guard the waterways leading to Lake Ponchartrain and New Orleans. Fish the canals that shoot off the main channels; spinnerbaits and other noisy lures work well. (Specific information about kayak fishing Shell Beach will come in the next specific site location description.)

A Little Fish Story

I was freezing. No, I mean it; I felt like I was freezing to death. Late November on the Louisiana coast is not supposed to be this cold.

I had been looking forward for a long time to this three-day/three-night trip on the *Southern Way*—a massive, palatial powerboat—while it was docked way out in the middle of Biloxi Marsh. But here it was, blowing like stink out of the north, and the duck hunters were happy. And I was freezing.

When I loaded my gear and old blue kayak on the transport pontoon barge at Shell Beach it was drizzling, and by the time we got way out in the marsh where the mothership was docked it was raining—hard. The wind had backed to the north and it was starting to come hard, too—it felt like straight from the North Pole.

The other folks on this particular trip were excited at this change in the weather. They were duck hunters, and this weather change meant the ducks would be coming in thick. I was not excited at all about the weather change. I liked the pleasant seventy-five-degree weather we'd had this winter up to this point.

Once arrived at the dock where the two big boats were secured we had a wonderful supper on the *Southern Way*. The three-man permanent crew are all Cajuns, you see, and Cajuns have a thing about good food and good eating. I slept well that night.

In the morning the duck hunters got up feeling even better. The chilly wind of yesterday evening had turned cold. Really cold. And it was still roaring.

As the duck hunters left I went down to my quarters and looked through my gear. I was grateful for remembering to put in my thin neoprene waders. I did not plan on getting in the water by any means, but wearing wet pants from paddling a kayak is no fun in cold weather like this. Waders are wonderful things to have in cold weather on a kayak. So I got my waders on, put on two hoodies, my PFD—for once I was happy to have the thick insulation of the flotation device around me—and went to try my luck. I shivered in the vicious, cold wind as I stepped out of the warm cabin of the mothership.

As the sun came up—it was a clear, cold day for sure—it sounded like a young war had started in Louisiana. Shotguns blasted from all directions and the ducks were taking a beating.

I got myself ready, eased carefully into my kayak, put the drive gear into place, and pedaled around the bows of the big boats to a small canal across the channel from our dock area.

To be honest, I did not expect much fishing today because of the wind and cold, but I had anticipated this trip too long to stay moping on the boat sulking because of the rotten fishing conditions.

I pedaled up the little feeder bayou and used a hand net to remove a live shrimp from my bait bucket—I was not about to put my bare hand into that cold water! I tossed the shrimp on a kahle hook-up close to the shore—he seemed glad to get back in the water and out of the cold air; he was freezing too. I watched my float for a minute and listened to the booming of the shotguns. When I glanced back my cork was gone.

Please, do not let me fall in! This was a very cold start to a great kayak fishing trip.

Yes, it appears Biloxi Marsh reds will bite even in cold weather.

A fool of a redfish had taken my shrimp and made a meal of it. I set the hook and brought the hard-fighting slot size red to the kayak. The Cajun crew had asked me to bring some reds back for grilling if I got lucky and actually caught some.

Now, how about this! Maybe these Biloxi Marsh reds don't care about the cold wind.

And they didn't. I pedaled my way up another connecting creek to a pond—maybe two hundred yards across—with a creek coming in one side and the creek I had moved up on the other.

This pond was full of reds. They were not super active. They were not chasing mullet or shrimp, and they sure weren't hitting topwater lures, but they would jump all over a jig and grub or a live shrimp put before them.

I caught reds all morning and the chill wind seemed to disappear—at least I did not notice it. And when I heard the duck hunters return I figured I would go see what they had done. I had my Louisiana limit of reds, much to the surprise of our Cajun hosts.

The guides and crew were busy cleaning the ducks gathered that morning, building fires in the grills, and getting water boiling over propane burners. I love eating with Cajuns.

We had "duck poppers," which are absolutely fresh duck breasts wrapped around a slice of onion and pepper marinated in some kind of magic Cajun sauce (I think it was Italian dressing, to tell the truth). The "duck poppers" were then fast-grilled over a hot bed of coals. We had grilled oysters on the half shell. We had grilled redfish with lots of Tony's seasoning liberally applied. This was perhaps the best lunch I had ever eaten.

For supper that night we had some grilled steaks—I do not know when I have ever had better steaks.

Did I mention that on these multi-day mothership kayak trips in Louisiana you can expect to eat very well?

A live shrimp or soft plastic jig was the ticket for great redfish action on Biloxi Marsh.

In the morning it was even colder and the wind had not dropped a bit, but I had a pretty good idea of what to do. I dressed up, loaded up, pedaled my way up the little creek, and the reds were still there. They were still hungry. I managed to find and catch some larger ten-to-twelve-pound reds on this day's fishing in the small pond. I even found a pair of reds actively chasing cold-slowed mullet in a little feeder creek mouth. I caught both of these fine fish on successive casts.

Just imagine what the fishing would have been like on a trip with "good" weather?

Special Considerations

A very good thing about fishing the Biloxi Marsh is that the fish bite year round. Even in the coolest winter weather redfish will still aggressively feed and can be targeted by kayak anglers. This means kayak anglers can schedule trips here around their calendars and still be confident they will have some fine fishing.

When fishing the marsh during duck season, kayak anglers need to be aware that there are lots of duck hunters in Louisiana, and they get upset when a kayak angler unknowingly paddles through their decoy spread, so keep an eye open for duck hunters and their gear.

Also, please be careful when paddling around catching redfish. It is very easy to get lost in the Biloxi Marsh, and even if you can still see the mothership off in the distance, it can be very confusing as to how to get back home. Most mothership operations give each angler a handheld VHF radio whenever they leave the big boat. This can surely make things better when it gets late and it is not clear how to get back home.

Local Sources of Information

Southern Way
www.southernwaycharters.com
601-466-0152

Pack and Paddle
Packpaddle.com
337-232-5854
601 Pinhook Road
Lafayette, Louisiana 70501

Great Kayak Fishing Site 15
Shell Beach, St. Bernard Parish, Louisiana

General Site Information

Shell Beach lies in a part of Louisiana that was very hard hit by Hurricanes Katrina and Isaac. The local area and the folks who live and work here suffered much damage from the storms. There is very limited close-by housing and short-term stay facilities, so visitors to this area may have to find places to stay in Chalmette, which is about twenty miles away from Shell Beach, but it is an easy, interesting drive over mostly rural roads to reach good kayak fishing. The Shell Beach area is mostly fished by locals, and that is a good recommendation; if the locals fish there that means the fishing is good.

A good thing for kayak anglers who come to visit and fish Shell Beach is that it is only a short drive—maybe forty-five minutes depending on traffic—from downtown New Orleans, and there are lots of places to stay in and around the Big Easy.

Anglers visiting Shell Beach will want to get all necessary food and supplies in Chalmette. Once at Shell Beach there are very few stores to buy anything other than live bait and some wonderful seafood fresh from the water.

At Shell Beach, kayak anglers will find good launch sites either at the very end of the road along Ysclosky Canal, where there is a small parking area, or at Frank Campo's Marina. Either of these launch sites will put kayak anglers in the marsh or on the old

Early morning working grass edges and shores can be very effective for redfish at Shell Beach.

Sunrise at Shell Beach is a wonderful time for kayak anglers to get out on the water.

pilings in Lake Borgne very quickly. Campo's Marina is a very good place to obtain live shrimp and other live bait—always a good bet when fishing the Gulf Coast.

When fishing Shell Beach kayak anglers can find some very good redfishing in the small creeks and bayous that feed into the larger canals in the marsh just out from Ysclosky Canal—which is where most kayak anglers put in. By the way, Ysclosky Canal is not the most attractive body of water in the world; it has lots of commercial fishing boats and docks along its length, but in winter reds and specks get in the canal very thick and kayak anglers can have a lot of fun catching these stacked up fish.

When launching at Shell Beach kayak anglers will see off in the distance a large structure. This is old Fort Beauregard—also called Fort Proctor—which was built before the Civil War to protect the waterway leading into Lake Pontchartrain and New Orleans. It was never really manned or supplied even during the war.

The area between the old fort and the launch sites is marshy, and it is a great place to find some good redfish action in the creeks.

Kayak anglers will see a large field of old pilings and other concrete structures in open water to the right as they exit the big canal toward Lake Borgne—the open body of water out past the old fort. There is a tall navigation structure off to the side of this field of pilings. These are the remains of old railroad and other commercial and military structures that have been abandoned. These pilings are prime places to find sheepshead

Old Fort Beauregard has been standing watch over Lake Borgne since before the Civil War.

in cooler weather and redfish and trout and flounder any time. It may take a bit of exploration to find the parts of the piling field that the fish are holding close to, but the fish are almost always there somewhere.

Lake Borgne lies out past the fort, and it is a massive body of water with lots of open water for specks and lots of marshes and bayous on the shorelines for reds.

For fishing Shell Beach—as well as most places on the Gulf Coast—look for moving water, either tide- or wind-generated. Look for bait moving in the water. This can be shrimp, small mullet, or pogies popping. Finally, look for birds diving and working. This almost always means fish.

How to Access the Area

This is not easy. It might be easier to use a GPS to reach Shell Beach from I-10, but here are basic driving directions. Keep in mind, the fishing at Shell Beach makes the navigation problems required to reach the area worth the effort. Once again, our best advice to visitors is *slow down*!

Kayak launching at Shell Beach is quite easy, and there is good parking at the lot at the end of the road.

From I-10, take the Chalmette exit I-510. Take a right and cross the Paris Road Bridge. Continue on until you intersect Hwy 39/Judge Perez Hwy.

Take a left on Hwy 39/Judge Perez Hwy and continue for quite a way through Chalmette. Pretty soon you will be out in bayou country. Cross the Violet Canal high rise bridge and continue until you reach Hwy 46. At the flashing light take a left on Hwy 46. Continue to the flashing light by a Junction Food Store and take a left at the food store. Continue on until you come to the Yscloskey Bridge. Cross the bridge and take the immediate left. Follow the bayou to Shell Beach, and Campo's Marina will be at the end of the road. I promise that after you drive this route once you will never forget it.

A Little Fish Story

My wife was having a fine day catching rat reds and small slot-size reds, and I was having a good day watching her catch fish. I would have had a better day if I had been catching fish, too, but I was just not having much luck. It was just one of those days.

We had launched earlier just after sunrise and then paddled across the open water of the channel—the Mississippi River Gulf Outlet—that separates the houses and seafood processing plants of Shell Beach and the wide expanses of the marsh where we had come to find redfish.

This is not the biggest redfish in the world, but even rat reds pull hard.

We had paddled our way up along the grassy shores of the bayou leading directly from Shell Beach to the open water of Lake Borgne and the little reds had responded to the live shrimp my wife offered them.

These little reds were gorgeous fish—golden bronze in color, with many of the fish showing extra spots of deep black rather than the standard issue single spot that redfish usually display on their tails. The reds were holding very tight to the shoreline, and the best places to catch them, according to my wife, were where grass and reeds were growing in the water.

I was not doing so well. I heard my wife yell to me to come look at her latest catch, so I paddled over, and there in my wife's hand was a fine two-pound bass. It seems that here at Shell Beach redfish and bass often will be found in the same areas eating the same thing. This bass was only the first of several that my wife caught while fishing for redfish.

And this was the way our morning went. My wife caught fish and I tried to catch fish.

Later that day, after we had returned to our lodgings for a meal and a little combat nap, I went back on the water and fished around some of the many rock jetties that help stabilize the eroding shorelines of the Shell Beach area and the change in scenery seemed to be working.

I began to catch some small speckled trout. These fish will be perfect for keeping and frying up in a few months, but they were too small to keep now. But at least I was catching some fish.

I tossed my ¼-oz. jig with a scented grub body up close to the lure-eating rocks of the jetty and started a slow hop-hop-hop retrieve. I got the jig close enough to my kayak for me to see the lure in the water and then things got a whole lot more interesting.

I saw a shadow charge my lure and then I saw the flash of a golden-bronze side as a redfish took my lure. At first I could not tell just how big this red was, but I soon got a good idea of what I had established connection with.

My spinning reel made a long, painful-sounding squeal and my line ripped through the water as a big redfish made a powerful run. When the run stopped the redfish gave me a series of head shakes which shook my hands gripped on the rod with each pump. This was a better redfish.

Then the red decided he was tired of playing with me and he made another long, powerful run. My reel's drag gave line, my rod bent way over, and I held on and tried to keep from messing up this fight.

It took me a while, but I finally got the red worked up close to the boat. This red was much better than anything else I had seen for a while. I let the fish make one more run away from me and then I pressured the fish to the side of the boat again.

This time the tired old red rolled over and I gently lifted the fish from the water. This red weighed between twelve and fifteen pounds. For someone else it would have been a twelve pounder. For me it was an easy fifteen.

Working the Shell Beach jetties for reds can be lots of fun.

Largemouth bass are often neighbors with Shell Beach reds, and they fight hard, too.

Here's what it is all about: kayak anglers have got to love those strong over-slot size reds.

I took a few pictures to prove my catch and then I eased the tired old red back into the water. It feebly moved its tail and then with a powerful thrust it was gone.

I love catching redfish from a kayak, and even on days when I just catch one, if it is the right one, that one is enough.

Special Considerations

Kayak anglers putting in at Shell Beach need to keep in mind this is a very active commercial fishing area, and it is not uncommon to see shrimp boats pulling nets just out from the Ysclosky Canal and other powerboats making their way at top speed to their fishing grounds. Kayak anglers need to keep an eye open and try to stay out of the way

Shell Beach is hurricane country. When the big storms come in people are lost, but not forgotten.

of larger commercial boats. Also lots of powerboat anglers use this area, and they may not be able to see a kayak ahead of them, especially in rough seas. Try to have a warning flag on your kayak and make sure you do not put yourself in close contact with larger boats.

A strong east wind can make launching and paddling the open water at Shell Beach a little tricky, but once in the marshes the wind becomes much less of a factor.

Be patient when driving through the Shell Beach area. Quite often drivers have to wait while delivery trucks for New Orleans restaurants and seafood markets are loaded with fresh seafood from commercial fishing boats.

Local Sources of Information
Frank Campo's Marina
1301 Yscloskey Hwy
St. Bernard, LA 70085
bcampo@aol.com

Great Kayak Fishing Site 16
Grand Isle, Lafouche Parish, Louisiana

Miles and miles of great roadside kayak fishing—Grand Isle is kayak fishing at its best.

Just ease your kayak along and work a lure down that shoreline, but you had better hold on to your rod.

General Site Information

Once a kayak angler arrives at Grand Isle it may be hard to keep their car on the road; there is just so much fishing water all around, and it all looks good. And here is the tough part: it all *is* very good for kayak fishing.

As the kayak angler drives off the ramp at the end of the elevated part of LA-1 and back on water-level roadways they will realize LA-1 is the only road out here; the world consists of the two lanes, a very few houses and stores along the road, and miles and miles of bayous, creeks, ditches, and open water. In most places in Grand Isle it is possible for a kayak angler to simply pull off the road in a safe place, unload the 'yak, and go fishing.

This is one of the best places in the world to find redfish that are willing and eager to hit topwater lures. There are rat reds, slot reds, and big old bull reds to be found all over Grand Isle waters. And in many spots no one but kayak anglers can get to the fish—there's lots of skinny, skinny water here.

During the winter speck trout load-up just south of LA-1, kayak anglers can have a ball catching these hard fighting, great tasting fish for a Cajun fish fry. Jigs and soft plastic white grubs are good lures for cold weather specks.

Some very big black drum also call Grand Isle home, and they will take a kayak angler for a slow speed, long distance kayak sleigh ride when hooked.

But it is the redfish that are the main attraction for kayak anglers. This is the place for a kayak angler to come when redfish caught on fly rod are the desired effect. The reds here are not spooky, and most of the time a competent kayak fly caster can get close enough to tailing and waking reds to get good casts. (When I can catch reds on the fly rod as I do at Grand Isle you can assume that the fish allow anglers to get close.)

There are live bait and tackle shops on the island, but there are no kayak supply and repair facilities close. Call our friends at Pack & Paddle up in Lafayette for needed gear, supplies, and advice.

There are very large reds to be found in Caminada Pass, but the currents can be strong; watch what is going on when fishing the pass, and watch for lots of larger commercial fishing and petroleum industry craft—it is a busy pass.

Grand Isle gives kayakers super easy access to wonderful fishing water.

How to Access the Area

This is a little complicated, but the destination is worth the struggle. This will take about two hours from New Orleans depending on traffic.

From I-10 in New Orleans take the Kenner Exit/Exit 220 on to Hwy 90/US 310. Stay on Hwy 90/US 310 through Destrehan, Boutte, and Des Allenade toward Raceland. From US 90/310 take exit 215B toward Raceland. At the end of the exit ramp take a left at the fork toward Lockport on LA 3085. Turn left on 3085 and go seventeen miles. LA 3085S becomes 15th Street, then cross the bridge across Bayou Lafourche. Turn left on to LA325 and go 15.5 miles to merge with LA 1-S. Continue on LA 1-S to Leeville. Turn right on the elevated LA 1-S Expressway (a toll is charged here). At the end of the elevated expressway turn left on to LA-1. Go ten miles to Grand Isle and you made it!

A Little Fish Story

One of the things I enjoy most about being an outdoor writer is that I get to take some great fishing trips to wonderful places, all as part of the job. I am not really having fun—I'm working—that is what I tell folks. And no, they don't believe me when I say that, either.

Grand Isle reds are always ready and willing to eat.

Big reds are common at Grand Isle, so kayak anglers need to come ready for a fight.

Our son Rob has a full-grown red hooked up and he is going for a kayak sleigh ride.

My son and I were scheduled to fish on a Saturday at Grand Isle—one of my favorite inshore places in the world—with Captain Danny Wray. Danny is a nice guy and a very good guide, and he knows the Grand Isle area very well.

My son and I arrived on Friday afternoon, got our motel arrangements made, and then we looked at each other. So, what do we do now? It is too early for supper and going to bed, and it's too late in the day for a major fishing expedition.

We decided to just hop back in the truck and cruise down Louisiana Highway 1 and look for a good place to pull off and drop the kayaks in for the last two hours of daylight. So we did just that.

We found a nice-looking creek that crossed the road and we parked the truck and quickly unloaded the kayaks and gear—isn't it nice about kayaks; it takes about

There is nothing quite like catching Grand Isle
redfish from a kayak—lots of fun.

seven minutes to go from packed and on the road to unloaded, repacked, and on
the water.

We paddled up the bayou against the falling tide until we came to a smaller side
bayou that looked good. I pedaled in first and my son followed, and that is why I saw
the redfish first. There, over against the farther shoreline was the unmistakable wake
of a redfish searching for its supper. I pedaled my kayak closer, and when I was in
casting distance I put the jig and grub about five feet in front of the red. The wake sped
up, the fish struck, and I had a late afternoon redfish fight on my hands.

This red was not big—maybe five pounds—but he was spirited, and he fought me
hard all the way back to the kayak. I admired this aggressive fish in the golden light of
the setting sun. Now this is the way to end a day.

I tried to show the red to my son but I could not see him or his kayak. I paddled
back to the main stream we had entered and there he was, but he was not alone. His
rod was bent way over and his kayak was being moved without him touching a paddle. I
pedaled over and watched him do a very good job fighting his fish, which was obviously
a lot bigger than the red I had caught.

The redfish slowly pulled his kayak up the bayou and under a tall set of powerlines
overhead, then the redfish stopped running and tried to bore deep in the center of
the stream.

My son worked the fish well, and before long the fine ten- or twelve-pound redfish
was finning alongside his little sit-in kayak. He carefully lifted the redfish for some

Many kayak clubs and groups make Grand Isle a favorite destination for trips because they catch lots of fish!

pictures, and with the last light of the day we both admired the redfish so typical of the reds at Grand Isle.

He put the tired red back home in the water and the fish jerked away and ran for freedom. Then we smiled at each other and made our way back to the truck before it got dark.

I was looking forward to the next day's fishing, but I doubted it could get much better than this.

Special Considerations

Grand Isle has several places for visiting kayak anglers to stay. If you are expecting swank and fancy it is not here. Basic, clean, affordable motels and condos are the rule. There are good seafood restaurants on the island, as would be expected.

The State Park at Grand Isle is a fine place for kayak anglers to stay if they are camper/tent equipped. Call and make reservations well ahead of time—the state park is a popular place.

Bugs can be a problem at Grand Isle, as at all Gulf Coast locations. Kayak anglers will need to have and use good insect repellent.

Now for some serious information. If you are driving a vehicle with an out-of-state license plate—*slow down*! This is no joke. The small towns of southern Louisiana are notorious for stopping out-of-state visitors and issuing speeding citations. If the speed limit is thirty-five you'd best be going thirty. Even if local Louisiana vehicles are moving faster than the speed limit, your out-of-state car will be the one that is pulled over. I have left a good deal of money in Louisiana through the years for speeding tickets. Also make sure you have up-to-date proof of insurance and registration in your vehicle.

On a happier note, in August, Grand Isle hosts the annual Ride the Bull Kayak Fishing Tournament, one of the largest kayak fishing tourneys in the world. Hundreds of kayakers work the strong currents at Caminada Pass for bull reds, and some very big ones usually come in to win this contest. There are also reported to be some pretty good after-tournament parties that go on—this is Louisiana after all.

Local Sources of Information
Calmwater Charters
Captain Danny Wray
225-721-8182

Pack & Paddle
337-232-5854
info@packpaddle.com

The good folks at Pack & Paddle are very knowledgeable and helpful for visiting kayak anglers. These folks fish southern Louisiana coastal waters a lot and they know their fishing. Also for any needed gear or equipment Pack & Paddle has the widest selection of kayak fishing hardware in Louisiana. These are good people to get to know.

Grand Isle State Park
985-787-2559
grandisle@crt.la.gov

Great Kayak Fishing Site 17
Cocodrie, Louisiana Terrebonne Parish

Open water specks at Cocodrie will be found under diving birds.

Sunset over Cocodrie bayous—some great fishing
today and better fishing tomorrow.

General Site Information

Cocodrie is famous for its inshore fishing for reds and specks. Although all of coastal Louisiana is good for these two game fish, Cocodrie just seems to have things a little better than many places.

Kayak anglers can look for places along the way to the actual settlement of Cocodrie to pull off and slide the kayak in for a little pre-arrival kayak fishing expedition. Many of the ponds and bayous visible from the road are very solid producers of reds in particular.

Specks are big at Cocodrie; kayak anglers can fish live shrimp under popping corks for fast action.

Cocodrie reds will be in every indentation in the shoreline. Work jigs, spoons, and spinners across the shoreline and hold on tight.

The larger, more open waters which can be easily accessed from the roadside as it enters Cocodrie are very good for specks. Look for flocks of diving birds working the open water. Most of the time specks will be under the birds, driving shrimp and small minnows to the surface where the birds can work them, too.

Kayak anglers can fish the larger streams and bayou, and where there is good tide current, some very big reds can be found and caught. Expect a kayak sleigh ride when one of these big bull reds comes to call.

If a trip with a guide can be arranged, and this is very possible, fishing around Timbalier Island, out where the Cocodrie inshore waters meet the gulf, can be very good, and some super-large reds and black drum can be found here.

As always, it is hard to beat a live shrimp fished under a popping cork, but I have had good luck at Cocodrie with simple jigs and scented soft plastic grub when casting to the feeding specks and along the shorelines of the bayous for reds. Gold spoons worked along shorelines can produce some very aggressive redfish strikes. For color selections of jigs and grubs it is hard to beat a black and chartreuse grub.

How to Access the Area

I doubt anyone has ever arrived at Cocodrie by accident. It is one of those "end of the road" places where people go on purpose. It will take about two hours to reach Cocodrie from New Orleans.

To reach Cocodrie, take I-10 at New Orleans and head west toward Baton Rouge. Merge on to I-310 S at exit 220 toward Boutte, Louisiana. Take US-90 W toward Houma, Louisiana. Take the LA-182

Some really big bull reds will be found in the major channels at Cocodrie.

Look for the birds at Cocodrie, because
the specks will be found under them.

exit toward Houma. Take a left on HW 182/LA-182. Turn left on HW 3087. Turn left on
E. Main—LA 24/LA 56—and stay on LA 56. Arrive at Cocodrie.

A Little Fish Story

It only took a moment for me to get excited. My son and I had just arrived at Cocodrie
with our kayaks—we had a big-boat trip scheduled the next morning with a guide to
catch some massive reds and black drums out in the gulf, but we had plenty of time
to get into fish catching trouble this sunny afternoon.

What got me excited was the big flock of birds screaming and diving over patches
of disturbed water out in the open bayou just off the one road coming into Cocodrie.

My son, being younger and stronger than I am, got his kayak to the action a bit
before I did. He hooked up with a hot speckled trout on his first cast. He worked the
fish to his kayak and admired it before he released it and cast again.

By then I had arrived on the scene of the crime—murder was being committed
on a widespread basis as specks killed and ate shrimp as fast as they could. I made a
short cast and my jig was immediately taken by a trout.

These schoolie trout were not huge fish—one to two pounds on average—but
they were very eager to bite any kind of lure presented to them and they fought hard
when hooked.

Finally the trout either got wise that something was going on or they just ate up
all of the shrimp. The school dispersed, the screaming birds left, and my son and I
floated on the smooth, windless surface. We then paddled our way to the nearest bayou
which fed into the open water.

This place just looked super fishy. There were good fairly deep waters close to the shorelines, and from time to time we could hear the particular sound a redfish makes when it eats something on the surface.

My son worked one bank and I took the other, and it only took a little while before we realized that this bayou not only looked fishy, it was fishy.

Reds were using the shoreline to help corral and control the mullet and shrimp they were chasing. A fairly long cast with a lure of almost any description would get the attention of the hungry reds.

I pitched an LSU colored jig and grub a long way up the shoreline and I only got it a few yards back toward me before the water boiled, mud rolled from the shallow bottom, and I had a good red on. This red fought hard like all Louisiana bayou reds do, and I was very pleased to finally get the eight- or nine-pounder to the boat for a quick set of photos.

We fished the sun down on Cocodrie, and as the sun began to touch the horizon I noticed that the local population of no-see-ums and mosquitoes had discovered me, and they were just as eager to bite me as the reds and specks had been to bite our lures.

We made a quick—and thankfully fairly short—paddle back to the launch point, jumped out, loaded the 'yaks in back, and drove down the road to CoCo Marina, where we had rooms for our trip.

After a first rate supper at the marina's restaurant we agreed that the next day—the "official" fishing trip—had a lot to do to match this first day's fishing. But it did, and that is fishing at Cocodrie.

Special Considerations

The name "Cocodrie" comes from the old Cajun word for alligator—and there are some serious gators found here. They will not bother kayak anglers, but they are impressive when viewed from a close distance.

Cocodrie has some impressive gators to see—from a distance.

There is not much in the way of non-fishing activities at Cocodrie; this is a fishing destination, and other forms of entertainment are very scarce. Visiting kayak anglers will want to call ahead and make reservations for overnight stays, especially during the heavy fishing pressure times of late spring, summer, and early fall. There are privately owned and operated fish camps and guide services at Cocodrie, but I can recommend the facilities at CoCo Marina very highly. Their restaurant is very good, there is a bar, guides can be arranged from there, and there is a pool and splash park for the kids. Do call and make arrangements before your trip—please do not assume there will be room at the inn.

Cocodrie waters are not hard to access; there are lots of good roadside places to pull off and get your kayak in the water.

Any special supplies and equipment needs should be tended to before arriving at Cocodrie—there's not much in the way of stores. There are some bait and tackle shops for fishing gear and bait.

Local Sources of Information

Pack and Paddle
info@packpaddle.com
337-232-5854

Captain Tray Collins
Kayak Fishing Louisiana
337-205-2018

CoCo Marina
www.cocomarina.com
800-648-2626

Great Kayak Fishing Site 18
Cypremort Point, St. Mary's Parish, Louisiana

General Site Information

Between Grand Isle and Cameron, if you want to access the gulf and coastal waters by car and kayak Cypremort Point is the only game in town.

Cypremort State Park offers day use facilities and some very good launch points. For kayak anglers who want to stay overnight there are six very nice cabins at the state park, but they rent out quickly, so make reservations way in advance to make sure a place to stay for a kayak trip to Cypremort is waiting.

The area around Cypremort has the standard range of Gulf Coast fish to be caught: reds and flounder are here for sure, but this is a great place for kayak anglers to come and find speckled trout. Especially later in the year specks can be thick in the channels and bayous, as well as in the open water of Vermilion Bay.

Kayak anglers can have good results with topwaters out in the open water of Vermillion Bay when the specks are chasing shrimp and driving them to the surface,

Open waters off Cypremort Park can be very
productive in fall for specks chasing shrimp.

but this is a prime place for anglers to use a cast net to obtain lots of good, fresh live bait. Pogies and shrimp can be expected, and a few good throws with a cast net can bring all of the best live bait possible—the stuff that lives there and that the trout are eating.

Captain Tray Collins guides kayak anglers in this area quite a bit when the conditions are right, and he recommends kayak anglers fish the area around the rock jetties. The channel between the jetties carries water of six feet or deeper, and this can be a very good place to find lots of specks and some very big ones, too.

Reds can be found in the marshes north of Cypremort Park as they hold near steep banks in the bayous.

When we get bird action such as these gulls there will be specks under them.

Kayak anglers will want to look at the State Park at Cypremort for good launch areas. The beach just south of the guard towers is a good spot, as is the beach past the campgrounds. Both ends—north and south—of the park allow kayaks to reach good fishing water fairly quickly. There are rock breakwaters and lots of oyster reefs for kayak anglers to fish.

How to Access the Area

This is not too hard. From I-10 take the exit on to US 90 and head south to LA 83. Continue south on LA 83, then turn right on LA 319. This road will take you into the park and the launch areas. As on all south Louisiana roads slow down, take your time, and look at the scenery.

A Little Fish Story

Cypremort State Park has two ends, and I could have chosen the upper end, which would have put me close to Shark Bayou and the more marshy type of fishing water. This is good water for reds and flounder.

But on this late fall morning I went to the lower end of the park so I could paddle across the Quintana Canal and put myself in open water near the long rock jetty protecting the shoreline of Vermilion Bay where Cypremort State Park lies. I was after some speckled trout for a fish fry that evening.

There was no wind on this late-arriving fall sunrise, and this made for perfect sight fishing conditions. In the fall at Cypremort, kayak anglers can almost always count on finding those best fish finders in the world—birds—as they work over schools of feeding specks.

On this calm morning I had no trouble launching my kayak and quickly making my way across the canal. This man-made access can be very busy on weekends, with lots of power boaters exiting the ramps and heading out to Vermilion Bay. Today I was the only angler of any kind here, and I liked the uncrowded and much less anxious conditions.

It is hard to beat the old classic jig and grub for speck trout on the Gulf Coast.

In the fall, lots of shrimp and other small tasty critters leave the Atchafalaya Basin swamps and bayous and head for the deeper, open water of Vermilion Bay and the gulf. This migration, as in many other parts of the Northern Gulf Coast, puts the big fish on their pre-winter feed, and it puts anglers in position to catch some good fish.

As I approached the long, low line of rock jetties I slow-trolled a jig and soft plastic grub behind my kayak. At this time of year kayak anglers will want something that they can cast a long way and which can be worked very slowly or very fast, depending on the fish they want. Jigs are perfect for this kind of fishing, and they are cheap, which is a good thing, because there is lots of gear-grabbing rough bottom structure to claim lures from anglers.

About a hundred yards ahead of me and perhaps fifty yards out from the jetty I saw a splash, and then another splash, and then I heard birds crying as they dove and worked the disturbed water. There were fish there, no doubt, and I sped up my paddle to get in casting distance. As I grabbed my rod and started to retrieve the jig for a cast something struck the jig, and my first trout of the day was soon in hand—a little ten-incher with dark spots and perfect silver sides. This was a pretty fish, but I wanted something a bit bigger for my fish fry fillets.

I stopped my movement about thirty yards short of the now constant splashes and rolls of feeding fish. My first cast into the feeding frenzy did not sink more than six inches before something gobbled up the jig and fought back against my rod's pressure. This fish was game, but it was small. I made another cast when this fish was removed from the hook and released, and once again a ten-incher came to hand.

Speck trout anglers learn one thing very fast: specks are schooling fish, and they tend to school according to size. Since I was after some larger specks to make bigger fillets I paddled around the feeding school of little specks and continued down the rock jetty. I could hear the enthusiastic splashes of the feeding small specks as I paddled a bit farther away from the rock structure of the jetty.

Specks come to the top to fight it out, and they fight hard.

Big specks put up a fine topwater fight, and they do not come in without a struggle.

Try a jig with a touch of pink—specks love pink lures of all kinds.

I saw a circling gull which dropped to the surface to pick up something to eat, and then I saw the spreading slick of oil rising to the surface of the water. Birds working and slick spreading—this spot deserved some attention.

I made a long cast toward the up-current side of the slick, and when the jig landed, I let it sink toward the bottom. As it found the bottom I started my retrieve and immediately I felt the pull-back of a much better fish. This was either a fair sized red or a dandy speck. And when the fine three-pound fish came to the surface and jumped and thrashed I knew I had my first keeper speck of the day on the line.

This fine, fat speck went into the soft-side cooler. I have been told that beauty is only skin deep, but speckled trout give that old story the lie. Specks are gorgeous fish when fresh from the water, and when properly cleaned and fried up right with just the right amount of seasoning specks are still beautiful fish, and they taste just as good as they look.

I moved back toward the spreading surface slick which told me where the school of bigger trout was making a breakfast of shrimp and minnows. I cast my jig and soft plastic grub tail into the slick and let the jig sink, but it didn't go far.

A sharp strike and take came, and another wonderful three-pound speck fought its way back to my kayak. This perfect eating size speck joined its friend in the ice bag.

It only took a half dozen casts into the feeding zone and I had all the specks I needed for supper. But nobody ever said I had to quit fishing when the fish were biting just because I had enough fish for supper.

So I did not stop, and I caught fine trout from that feeding school until I decided to make my way back to the launch spot and take my fish and I back to the cabin where we were having a first-rate Louisiana fish fry for supper.

And yes, it was some fine, good eatin' going on that night.

Special Considerations

Captain Tray Collins fishes the Cypremort area quite a bit, and he advises us that the level of the Atchafalaya River is crucial to fishing success at Cypremort. If the river is high the waters around Cypremort and Vermilion Bay will be muddy, and they will be fresh. This really slows down the fishing, especially for specks, reds, and other saltwater fish. The water needs to be at least seven parts per million of salt, and more salt is better for fishing.

The later part of the year is best for Cypremort kayak fishing. January and February are both good, since the water tends to be lower, cooler, and saltier—all good things for anglers. March through July can be tough, with high water and fresh water cutting down on the numbers and size of saltwater fish present.

Flood waters bring a rise on the Atchafalaya at any time of the year and can bring fishing to a halt until the water goes down. After the upstate floods of 2016, Cypremort late summer/early fall fishing was tough.

Local Sources of Information

Captain Tray Collins
Kayak Fishing Louisiana Charters
tray@kayakfishinglouisiana.com
337-591-6434

Pack & Paddle
337-232-5854
info@packpaddle.com

Great Kayak Fishing Site 19

West Cove-Lake Calcasieu, Cameron Parish, Louisiana

West Cove reds fight hard—just like all Gulf Coast reds. They do not quit quickly.

When we find birds working like this it is certain fish are feeding below.

General Site Information

West Cove can provide some excellent redfish for kayak anglers, especially when there is good tide movement. Water either moving in or out will often make for the best fishing here.

The canal leading from the boat launch on Highway LA 275 south of Sulphur, Louisiana, can be quite good for flounder—live bait such as finger mullet and bull minnows are best for the flat fish. Work these on the bottom on a Carolina rig with just enough weight to get the bait on the bottom; there is a lot of stuff on the bottom that will cost terminal tackle if too much weight is used.

Before the marsh that lies off the south shore of the canal—there are two main bayous leading from this marsh to the canal—is closed in October for the use of migrating water birds, the bayous there can be very good for reds. Look for places where smaller bayous and creeks feed into the main bayous and work these junction spots with jigs and gold spoons. Look for actively tailing and waking reds along the shorelines.

Gold spoons are very effective for reds on Lake Calcasieu, and they can be pulled through very rough territory.

Once a kayaker reaches the open water of West Cove—it is a big body of open water—things get interesting. West Cove is a very good place to find some hot speckled trout. There are worlds of oyster reefs and sandbars in West Cove—definite hazards for powerboats, but no concern for kayaks—and these reefs and bars are speck magnets. Look for splashes, and especially look for feeding birds. Specks will be under the birds. Jigs which can be cast a long way can be very effective for these open water specks, as well as heavy hard plastic swim baits.

Of course redfish will be on the bars and reefs, too, and they can be very active when a tide is moving water over the structure. When using live bait do not be surprised when a big ugly black drum takes a shrimp intended for specks or reds and provides a low-gear, very powerful fight. Black drums get very big and they are fun to catch.

Kayakers must be aware that a strong east wind can kick up a powerful chop on West cove that can make fishing tough. When the wind is really ripping from the east it might be the best idea to relocate to the other side of the lake and fish the protected shore.

How to Access the Area

Getting to West Cove from I-10 is not too difficult. Local traffic is generally quite light, and kayak anglers should not find much trouble getting to the best launch areas. Be aware that even though the Texas state line is very close you are still in Louisiana, so watch your speed.

To reach West Cove from I-10 Sulphur, Louisiana, take exit 20 toward Cameron. Turn left at Ruth Street and go a little more than two miles. Continue on to LA-108 and LA 275 for about twenty-five miles. Look for the brown and white West Cove Public Boat Launch signs. Follow the directions given. There are two boat launches at West Cove, and the launch closer to the lake is the better one for kayakers.

Here's a perfect West Cove slot red. This fish will make a great supper later.

A Little Fish Story

I do love calm, flat-water mornings when I am fishing on the Gulf Coast, and this morning on West Cove at Lake Calcasieu, in southwest Louisiana, is a perfect morning. The sun is starting to brighten up the eastern shore a long way off in the distance, and I am slowly paddling my kayak away from the launch point just off Hwy 275. It seems to me a loud noise would break and shatter the morning. It seems proper that I am not in a loud, disruptive powerboat on this quiet morning—just one reason that kayak fishing is such a wonderful way to spend my fishing time.

A flight of early fall teal whistle through the air overhead as they speed their way to their safe haven winter holding grounds in the marsh just south of the canal/bayou I am paddling down.

And then, as I make my way down the canal close to the shoreline fronting the marsh and its skinny water, I see another really good reason I should be fishing from a kayak. There is the absolutely unmistakable bulge and swirl of a redfish making a meal of a shrimp at the surface. It is a funny thing, but quite often, it is impossible to tell the size of a surface-feeding red from the disturbance it makes when it feeds. I have seen some really big reds make the gentlest sips as they take a mullet or shrimp.

But this fish is not alone. I see the water bulge and swirl as other redfish are formed in a feeding school.

At times like this it is important to keep in mind that when reds are schooled up there are lots of eyes to see danger approach, so I decide to hold well off at the outside of my casting range and try to work the edges of the feeding school.

I send a long cast ahead and to the side of the main body of feeding reds. I want to hook a fish, but I would prefer to not have to work a hooked red right through the middle of the school and spook all of them.

I slowly start the retrieve of my favorite old topwater plug—a pink and white scratched and scarred lure that has tempted many redfish over the years.

Once again the pink and white plug does its work well. There is a splash as a good red takes the plug and the hooks bite and hold, and the red makes a powerful run with a very impressive wake away from the main school of feeding reds.

I am able to keep good pressure on the red, and as good-sized reds always do it pulls me and my kayak on a slow ride. And this is another good reason to fish from a kayak—being so light and easy to move, kayaks keep big fish from ever getting a harsh, line-breaking pull when they run hard. The red and I have a good time—at least I do—and then I have the nice eight-pounder at boat side. A few quick pictures and the fish is gone.

But I can see the school of reds that my fish came from off in the distance. There is the slightest little chop starting now from a morning breeze that is coming with the rising of the sun.

I paddle my way back to casting distance and I make another long range cast toward the feeding reds.

This time I don't even have a chance to move the lure at all—something absolutely blasts the plug and makes a violent run right though the school of reds. The

The marsh at West Cove is a fine place, but remember it is off limits for entry after October.

water's surface is shattered by the wakes of spooked reds going in all directions, but I've got more to worry about than finding this scattered school of reds again.

This hooked red is a much bigger fish than the first one I caught. This red just powers line off the level-wind reel I am using, and I hope the twenty-five-lb. test braid line and thirty-lb. fluorocarbon leader are stout enough for this fish.

My kayak is being pulled at a good pace down the canal toward the open waters of West Cove, and all I can do is hold on and let the reel's drag and the light weight of my kayak do their work. I can feel the powerful head shakes of the red as it struggles against the pressure of my line.

The big red makes another run. Line is ripped from my reel and my rod bends way over. And then the rod snaps up straight and dead. I reel in my limp and weak line and the leader shows where the knot gave way. My old favorite lure is gone, lost to a big, big fish.

But when I think about it, that is not a bad way for an old favorite to meet its end—doing what it is supposed to do and doing it well.

I tie on another lure—maybe it will be my new old favorite—and I look to find another West Cove redfish.

Special Considerations

The marsh area of West cove is closed October–March to protect migratory birds—a very good idea. Even though the area is full of redfish, stay out of the posted marsh area during the closed months.

If fishing the open water of West Cove, be aware that a strong wind with any kind of easterly component can make for some very rough water. The open part of this area is wide open, and rough seas can build quickly with east winds. The marsh areas are much better choices when the wind is ripping here.

Although there are a few marinas and lodges in the West Cove area, most kayak anglers will want to look for housing in either Sulphur, off the interstate, or in Lake Charles.

Local Sources of Information

Captain Tray Collins
Kayak Fishing Louisiana Charters
tray@kayakfishing Louisiana.com
337-591-6434

Pack and Paddle
337-232-5854
info@packpaddle.com

Those small creeks off the main bayous at West Cove
are prime places to find hungry, aggressive reds.

Notes